Courtesy of *Herald & Review*

On behalf of the officers and staff of
First of America Bank, we offer our sincere
thanks to the people whose hard work,
enthusiasm and love of history have preserved
Decatur's heritage and traditions.
We are pleased to present
Decatur Business: A Pictorial History,
the first in a series of four books on
the history of our community.

First of America Bank is proud
to have played a major role in the
development of Decatur over the years.
It is with this same pride we bring you
this handsomely illustrated and well-
documented volume. We are certain it
will prove to be a valuable addition to
your family library and a rare
collector's item in the future.

Phillip C. Wise
Community President
First of America Bank-Illinois, N.A.

On behalf of the officers and staff of
First of America Bank, we offer our sincere
thanks to the people whose hard work,
enthusiasm and love of history have preserved
Decatur's heritage and traditions.
We are pleased to present
Decatur Business: A Pictorial History,
the first in a series of four books on
the history of our community.

First of America Bank is proud
to have played a major role in the
development of Decatur over the years.
It is with this same pride we bring you
this handsomely illustrated and well-
documented volume. We are certain it
will prove to be a valuable addition to
your family library and a rare
collector's item in the future.

Phillip C. Wise
Community President
First of America Bank-Illinois, N.A.

Courtesy of *Herald & Review*

Decatur
Business
A Pictorial History

By

Karen Anderson

Dayle Cochran Merideth

G. Bradley Publishing, Inc.   **461 Des Peres Road**   **St. Louis, MO 63131**

Decatur Business

A Pictorial History

by Karen Anderson
Dayle Cochran Merideth

A limited edition of 3,000

PUBLICATION STAFF:

Authors: Karen Anderson
Dayle Cochran Merideth
Cover Artist: Larry Wetherholt
Book Design: Diane Kramer
Electronic Photo Editor: Michael E. Bruner
Copy Editor: Gloria Baraks
Publisher: G. Bradley Publishing, Inc.
Sponsor: First of America Bank-Illinois, N.A.

Table of Contents

Photos courtesy of *Herald & Review:* pages 5, 64, 77TL, 106T, 107TR, 111B, 152-153, back end sheet. Photos courtesy of Macon County Historical Society: pages 101T, 101B, 120-121, 156M, 156B, 157T.

ISBN-0-943963-49-4
PRINTED IN THE UNITED STATES OF AMERICA

Foreword

When Leonard and Alice Stevens and their eleven children gathered at the center of what would become Macon County in 1822 their task was to form a community that would epitomize the America they knew and loved and to make the unfamiliar landscape a meaningful place. They wanted to be at home.

Times were tough and challenging for the Stevens as well as for the families that followed. Take the reminiscences of pioneer, Marilla Martin Baker, as she wrote home to Tennessee in 1829. "We have no preacher, no doctor, no grist mill or saw mill, no cotten gin nor tan yard, but I hope we will lack none of these things long."

The soggy land upon which Decatur was built was once vividly described as "one vast pond where the mud turtle and water moccasin luxuriated, the mosquito wound his bugle, and the frogs gave a rival symphony."

From its swamplike beginnings to becoming a humble stop on the Great Western (later the Wabash) and the Illinois Central routes, the cluster of buildings soon grew into a cowtown of square storefronts with horses and wagons hitched next to the wood-planked sidewalks.

Commerce also was beginning to take shape. Instead of cash most goods were acquired in trade because there was not a lot of cash to go around. In the pioneer stores pork, pelts, cowhides, eggs, wild game and geese were brought in to trade for coffee, tea, a dining table, augers and axes or even a coffin for a baby girl.

The fact that the Sangamon River was not navigable was, without a doubt, a serious blow as the farmers had no market for their produce and transportation, in general, remained an obstacle to increased settlement.

Irregardless, the Decatur firsts kept coming: The Macon House was the first notable hotel established in 1839 and would later accommodate Lincoln, Douglas, Governor Oglesby and David Davis, a well-known circuit riding judge. The first big industry was the Rolling Mill that produced railroad iron in 1871 and demanded the skills of 400 men in the east part of the city: "a real boom business."

Progress also came in the form of the Priest Streetcar. That momentous day when "it seemed that the muddy gulf between the Old Square and the railroad station had finally been forever spanned." Soon thereafter, trolleys clanged into a charming late-Victorian city with Water Street businesses, city utilities, parks and confectioneries.

First and foremost in Decatur business came the long line of illustrious inventors who put Decatur on the map of the industrial world. Mueller, the Haworths, Hill, Beall, Faries, Cash, Smith and King, to name a few. The inventions: the world famous check rower, the hog ringer, the power corn sheller, the water-tapping machine, much valuable milling machinery, wire mate streetcar trucks, valves for submarines, fly-swatters, automatic grain weighers and a pencil sharpener.

A number of the implements used to plant and harvest the grain were invented locally, making Decatur a natural as a grain processing center. The spectacular success of A. E. Staley Manufacturing Company drew two major grain processors to Decatur: Spencer Kellogg and Archer Daniels Midland. With these three heavy industrial hitters within her borders, Decatur earned the title of "world soybean capital." In addition to grain processing, other sizable industries chose to make or keep Decatur home for their manufactories: Mueller, Shellabarger, Wagner, Chambers, Bering & Quinlan, Caterpillar, Firestone, General Electric, Polar, Heinkel, Traver Supply and Illinois Power are a few of those who have added their piece to the quiltwork of Decatur business and industry. Decatur also served as a furniture and garment manufacturing center, adding even more diversity to the industrial climate of the town.

The growth of Decatur is not only the result of heavy industry success, but the area has also grown because of the quality and expertise of the retail and service businesses along Decatur's main transportation arteries, Interstate 72 and Highway 51.

By combining text, documents, remembrances and quotations with a pictorial narrative one can look back at Decatur's history of business and industry. New faces and new technologies will likely bring additional challenges, but by looking at the past Decatur citizens can be reassured that the accomplishments and adaptability of earlier generations has prepared the community well for the changeable future.

The value to the reader will, in large measure, depend on that person's sense of relationship to the city. But hopefully all who look into *Decatur Business: A Pictorial History* will find that Decatur's past is more fascinating and meaningful than they had imagined.

In his *Story of Decatur,* E. B. Hitchcock quoted an unknown source describing this area: "Stretching in every direction were vast prairies covered with grass taller than a man, and growing as thick as the hair on a dog's back."

The city of Decatur was carved out of these prairie lands that were formed as the result of the Pleistocene North American ice sheet which extended into the midwestern United States almost to the junction of the Mississippi and Ohio rivers. The Pleistocene epoch ended 10,000 to 11,000 years ago leaving behind the fertile soil of central Illinois.

The glaciers left most of the area flat, with gently rolling areas along the waterways. Timber lined the Sangamon River and Big Creek in an area two to three miles wide with a narrower band near Friends Creek. The land consisted of black, rich soil from three to ten feet deep, which was a draw to settlers along with the abundant water, especially the Sangamon River.

Early settlements were established by Leonard Stevens and John Ward. Research indicates that Leonard and Alice Stevens were the first settlers accompanied by their children, Buel and Joseph. The Stevens settlement, established in 1821 or 1822 depending on the source consulted, was located three miles northwest of Decatur near the creek that now bears his name. John and Jane Ward came in 1824 and moved into an area south of the Sangamon River, buying the "improvements" of William Downing who had come in 1820 (taking over the Lorton fur trapper's cabin) to trap and gather honey. Members of the two settlements were not always on the best of terms.

By 1828, local settlers, encouraged by population growth, decided to request the formation of their own county. To this end Benjamin Austin, Andrew Smith and John Ward traveled to the state capital in Vandalia in January 1829, to seek passage of an act that would divide up Shelby County and form a new county. Such an act was approved on January 19, 1829, and Macon County was born.

Macon County was named for the Honorable Nathaniel Macon of North Carolina, a hero of the era. He had served in the army during the Revolutionary War, and had refused compensation for his services. He was elected to the state senate even before he left the army, and served in that capacity until 1785. Macon was then elected to the lower house of Congress in 1791, and remained there until 1815, serving also as Speaker from 1801 until 1806. From there he went to the United States Senate, in 1816, where he completed his term in 1828.

Included in the act to form Macon County was the provision to establish a county seat to be called the town of Decatur. At that time Shelbyville was the closest seat of justice, necessitating long trips over rivers and muddy roads for every legal transaction in the region.

The city of Decatur was named for one of the country's first naval officers, Stephen Decatur. Born in Worcester County, Maryland, January 5, 1779, Decatur served with distinction in the war with Tripoli and the Algerine War. Following his active naval career, Decatur was appointed Commissioner of the Navy. His life came to an abrupt end on March 22, 1820, in a duel of honor.

Stevens Creek in 1880. Photo taken just north of the old P D & E Railroad bridge. This is how Stevens Creek may have looked in pioneer days. (The P D & E- Peoria, Decatur, and Evansville later became the Illinois Central).

Joseph Stevens, a son of Leonard Stevens, was one of the earliest settlers in Macon County.

This 1930 photo shows the site of Leonard Stevens' cabin. It was located three miles northwest of Decatur.

Decatur was the pride of his country (and of Southerners, many of whom settled this area), and Decatur was a fitting name for a growing young city in the "West."

A commission was appointed to fix the location of the new county seat. Members included John Fleming, Jesse Rhoads and Easton Whitten, who met at the home of James Ward and were sworn before a justice of the peace to faithfully and impartially discharge the duties assigned to them. They did this, reporting their findings to the county commissioners' court and setting their hands and seals to the document on April 10, 1829, the same day on which they met and were sworn in. According to the commission's report, having impartially judged and viewed the present situation, with an eye to the future, the county seat was located "on the fifteenth section of township 16, north, in range two east, and the northeast quarter and the east half of said quarter."

All, however, may not really have been so easily and amicably settled. E. T. Coleman in his *History of Decatur and Macon County* suggested the possibility of another version of this story:

"Another report for whose accuracy we can not vouch but which at least seems quite plausible indicates that the determination of this site was not quite the simple matter that the official report indicates. There were several locations proposed and the final decision was passed up to the voters. At the first meeting of the settlers called to fix the site a majority voted to make the center of it a point on the east side of North Water Street and between North and Eldorado streets. This would have missed entirely the original town of Decatur as it was finally platted. The decision provoked much ill-feeling among the settlers south of the river, who numbered twenty-one more legal voters than there were north of the river at that time.

A second meeting was called, at which the former decision was recalled. A majority of those present were in favor of locating the town site south of the river on the highlands of Captain David L. Allen.

Before action could be taken, however, the meeting broke up in a free-for-all fight and one man was so badly beaten that he died.

A third meeting was held and the present Lincoln Square was chosen as the site center and the original town was so platted.

Evidently some of the south side voting majority was not present to be counted at the first meeting and by that failure Decatur is on the north side of the Sangamon instead of the south."

Whichever version is correct, the site chosen for Decatur was just a few miles from being in the exact geographical center of the county that is located in the geographical center of the State of Illinois. Benjamin Austin, Macon County surveyor, was paid the sum of $25 to lay out the town of Decatur based on the design of Shelbyville. Austin returned a complete plat to the commissioners of the court by July 1, 1830.

Decatur was originally laid out around a central square, which is now Lincoln Square. Four streets formed the edges of the city: Prairie on the north, Water on the east, Wood on the south, and Church on the west. Two streets called Main divided the city east and west and north and south.

Lots were ordered sold from the twenty-acre tract beginning on July 10, 1829. Initial sales were slow. James Renshaw gave Decatur an economic boost by purchasing land on Main Street and building the city's

Commodore Stephen Decatur, the naval hero for whom the town was named.

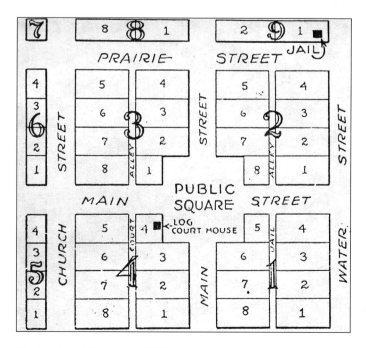

Early plat of Decatur. William A. Austin helped his brother, Benjamin, plat the town.

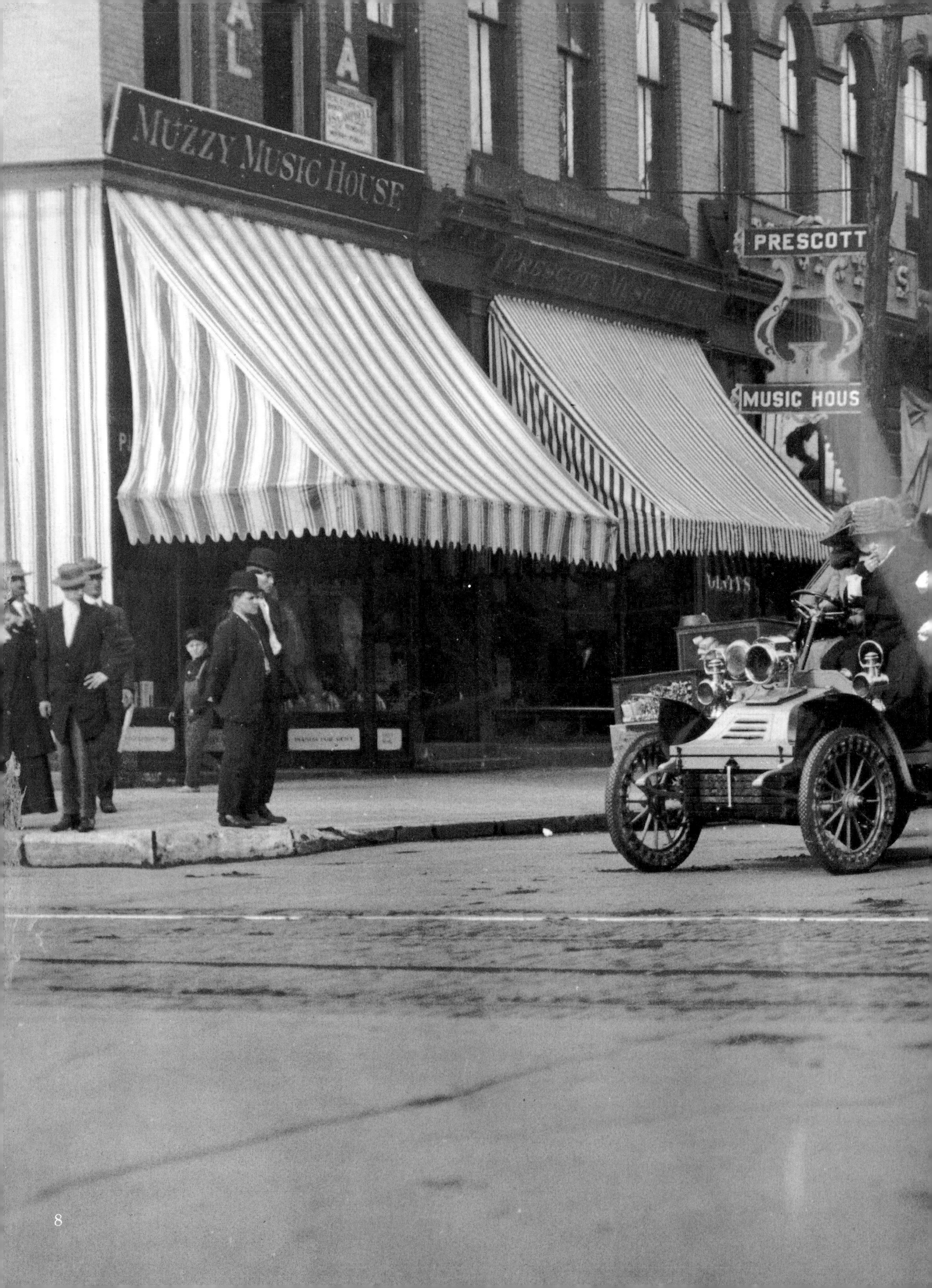
MUZZY MUSIC HOUSE
PRESCOTT
MUSIC HOUS

A horse scared from one of the city's first noisy "horseless contraptions" on the 200 block of North Main circa 1905. The Muzzy family owned the Prescott Music House according to the 1906 Decatur City Directory.

first tavern and store.

Provisions were also made in the act for raising revenues to cover county expenses. Smith's *History of Macon County* reports that a ..."tax of one-half per cent be levied upon the following personal property, to-wit: On slaves and indentured or registered negro or mulatto servants; on pleasure carriages; on distilleries; on stock in trade; on all horses, mares, mules or asses, and neat cattle over three years old; and on watches, with their appendages, and on all other personal property except the lawful fire-arms of each individual."

Every business had to be licensed before opening its doors. Licensing fees ranged from three to five dollars. The court also established fees for river ferries.

One would think that a town created in the middle of a prosperous and growing state, with the added advantage of having some of the most fertile land in the world, would have grown quickly. This, however, was not the case with Decatur, because there were also some drawbacks to the location, a major one being the Sangamon River. It was both boon and bane for the young town. A source of water is important for any settlement, and the Sangamon was, of course, a draw to original settlers. But it was not navigable. In an era when most transportation was by way of the water routes, this was a distinct disadvantage. There were early attempts to clear it of much of the debris that made traveling it almost impossible, but most of them were to no avail.

Roads were still almost nonexistent, and a major one, the Springfield to Paris road, bypassed Decatur to the south. It has been said that the major Indian trails also did not cross the Macon County area. There was, to be sure, some Indian activity here, game being quite abundant, but the important traveling routes mostly went all around and not directly through. The *Atlas of the Great Lakes* edited by Helen Hornbeck Tanner shows no Indian villages close to Decatur. Other sources, such as E. T. Coleman, report that Indians came through the area on a seasonal basis to do business with the Lorton trading post. After 1828, very few Indians were seen in the vicinity. Until the railroads came through Decatur in 1854, the town's growth remained static.

Another reason for this retarded growth was known as the "Illinois Shakes." Malaria by any other name is still miserable. Many new settlers went through the malaria season only once, then they packed up and returned to their former homes. Could the presence of malaria be wondered at when anywhere on the prairie little mud towers of crawfish could be seen? The custom of the immigrants of drinking from these crawfish holes with the aid of hollow reeds gave Illinois the nickname "Sucker State." There were, naturally, hordes of mosquitos. People refused to come and settle here, and an immigrant who happened to stop in a vicinity afflicted with the disease did not usually tarry long. It was also a seasonal affliction, not one in which an epidemic sweeps through and passes away, but one that had to be endured year after year. Quinine was bought by the pound. Malaria did not disappear until a general system of farm drainage was used to drain the land. It was intended to increase production of the farms rather than improve health, but it accomplished both.

This system of drainage was done by tiling, the tiles being made from the clay found in the area, and used to drain the wet, marshy ground. This was in fact one of Decatur's first industries.

Such was the beginning of Decatur. From an idea to a plat to a few buildings, Decatur began slowly to grow and develop. More businesses and industries were established as more people came and needs became evident. Increased population meant an increase in businesses. And, with the coming of the railroad, the town began its boom.

Left: The Sangamon River in 1914. Right: The Sangamon River channel in 1926.

Reminiscences

Work and Leisure

"I do not know that the hardships of the first settlers have been exaggerated but they have certainly been set out in undue proportion. The real pioneers had more leisure than we, their sons and grandsons, have today. The head of the family built the house with his own hands, it is true, but it did not take him as long as it does to get a house built today. To be sure there was at the first not a foot of sawed lumber in it, but neither was there in the house of his neighbor, so he had the comfort of being in the fashion. After the few acres of corn were laid by, the wheat harvested and trampled out, and the flax in the flax-pen, there was nothing more to do during the glorious months of the fall but to hunt and fish and visit the neighbors and attend camp meetings if religiously inclined. Horse races and shooting matches furnished plenty of excitement for those who were not religiously inclined.

In the winter there was but little to do except to keep wood cut to supply the all-consuming fireplaces and to get in the small acreage of splendid corn. This latter, following the southern custom, was considered a winter job till the winter of the deep snow kept nearly the whole crop buried until spring and suggested the wisdom of earlier harvesting."
[a quote from Rev. N.M. Baker in E. B. Hitchcock's Story of Decatur]

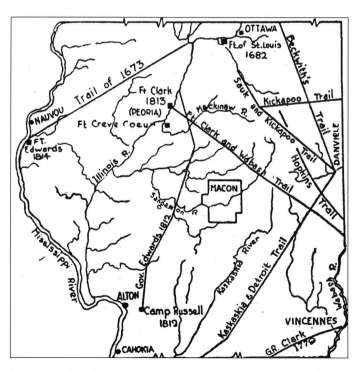

Indian Trails: Decatur supposedly was not on any major trails, but Indians did come through the area regularly.

Typical Settlers

John W. Smith's own family was typical of the settlers of that part of Macon county.

Robert Smith, grandfather of the historian, was the oldest of the family to come to Illinois and to Macon county. He was born in Guilford county, North Carolina, in 1782. His father, the great-grandfather of the historian, fought in the Revolution and was captured by the British in North Carolina. He removed to Tennessee with his family in 1803 and remained there until his death.

Young Robert fought with General Andrew Jackson at the Battle of New Orleans. He married and moved to Illinois, settling first in Sangamon county, coming to Macon county in 1828. He settled about six miles southwest of Decatur. One of his numerous family was a son, William C. Smith, who was born in Rutherford county, Tenn., in 1819. He removed with his people to Illinois, first to Sangamon county and later to Macon. [E. B. Hitchcock, Story of Decatur]

No Indian Depredations

There is no tradition or physical evidence that there was ever an Indian depredation, battle or massacre in the county. The Indians that were here after the settlement of the county began were on their way. There is tradition and some physical evidence that Indians were here in considerable number along the south bank of the Sangamon opposite Decatur, at the Indian camp ground on Hockaday farm, about Sulphur Springs near Mt. Zion and perhaps at Boiling Springs near the Dan Good farm in Hickory Point township and at the site of Dantown in Friends Creek township. There is no convincing evidence that there was ever an Indian village in the present limits of the county. Apparently they did not live here. They came here to hunt and fish and trap. There was an Indian trail that crossed the Sangamon river near the site of Lawton's and this became a public road, to disappear finally. [E.T. Coleman, History of Macon County]

Came in 1829

Christopher Miller and his wife, Betsy, who spent the last forty years of her life in Iowa, totally blind and lived to the age of 110, came by ox-wagon from Grayson county, Kentucky in 1829 (to Decatur) bringing with them their sons, William and James, and others of their eleven children then born. (The Miller uncle drove a stage coach.) Best of all for the Miller children ...was to go over to the stage stand on Christmas and hang up their Christmas stockings. [E.T. Coleman]

CHAPTER 2: TRANSPORTATION

In the normal course of settlement, immigrants followed the roads to wherever they were going. This was not generally the case in central Illinois, however. The Ohio River was a major "highway" for travelers to Illinois in the early years of settlement. As a result, many of the earliest settlers came from the southern states. Settlement away from the rivers was slow due to the many obstacles people faced in trying to get to the interior. In many places, the prairies were so marshy and infested with flies and other insects that the settlers were compelled to travel only at night. Modes of travel consisted mainly of horses and by foot. Roads were nonexistent, and even the trails were useless through much of the year. What passed for trails were no more than paths, some of which were really only lines marked by a tree branch having been dragged along the ground to point the way. These paths were without bridges, wound through country almost devoid of human habitation, and were muddy quagmires during part of the year. Many of these had been Indian trails, and were later followed by the stage coach routes, railroads and paved roads. Many of today's highways follow routes that the Indians traveled long ago.

In the early 1800s it was thought that the prairies could never be cultivated, and the expense of maintaining roads would be too burdensome to be worthwhile. But, when the area here began to be settled, it became apparent that roads would need to be developed. With an eye to this need, in 1829, the same year the county was formed, Benjamin Wilson, James Miller and Elisha Freeman, as county commissioners, divided the county into two road districts. William Hanks was road supervisor of District 1, north of the Sangamon River, and John McMennamy was supervisor of District 2, south of the river. William Ward, James Ward and Robert Smith were appointed road viewers. It was their job to determine if, and where, roads were necessary. These roads were still little more than dirt paths, and had little maintenance.

The Springfield road, known to travelers as "the government road" actually ran south of the Sangamon River through the Mount Gilead neighborhood. Travelers from the East and from Kentucky came into the area by this route. It is likely that if the railroads had not made an intersection in Decatur, a movement south would have taken the town south across the river.

Sometime during the 1830s stage coaches were in

The Wabash Railroad Depot in the early 1900s. Note the special carnival car in right foreground.

use on this route. There was a stop near Decatur known as the "Warnick Tavern," an elaborate log house built by William Warnick, Macon County's first sheriff. It was well enough known that it maintained the same name through several changes in ownership. By about 1840, there was a stage stand (a tavern where a driver could get a change of horses and where travelers could spend the night) operating evidently in what is now the Wyckles Corner area on the north side of old U.S. Route 36. It was said to have been built by Christopher Miller whose nephew, Abraham, drove the Springfield to Paris stage from 1840 until 1858.

The first regular stage service was between Decatur and Springfield, and it ran on a weekly schedule. Leonard Ashton, whose livery stable was located on the alley back of the Parlor Market, northeast of what is now Lincoln Square, did his best to keep the schedule and used to boast that his stage was never more than a week late even in the worst weather.

But the stage coach was never a popular mode of travel in central Illinois due to the bad roads. Passengers often had to walk a good part of their trip, even when the stages were running, and sometimes earned their tickets by prying the coach out of the mud with fence rails. At times, the heavy stages had to be abandoned altogether and a box-like wagon on two wheels was substituted so mail and important supplies could get through.

There was great pressure to develop some other kind of transportation system that might be more reliable. The rich soil of the area was the major draw to settlers, but there was little incentive for farmers to take advantage of the possibilities of that soil to grow more than they could consume themselves because there was virtually no way to get any surplus to market. An attempt was made to clear the Sangamon River for navigation by flatboat, but the venture was not successful. Goods were taken to market by wagon, which was both costly and time consuming. Little by little improvements were being made to the roads.

In addition to travel between towns, movement within the newly established county seat was also a growing need. A local hack service was necessary for short trips in and around the city. Livery stable operators met this demand. The first of these was James D. Tacit, who first walked to Decatur from Springfield with the tools of his trade on his back. In 1895, Byrd L. Davis, Sr. opened what was probably the best known of Decatur's livery stables.

After 1854, when railroad service began, the stage coach business gradually disappeared. Hack service continued within the city but eventually evolved into taxi service. In addition to hack service, there also came the streetcars. A charter for the first streetcar line was awarded by the city council on November 14, 1876. The first cars were drawn by horses or mules, but this was also true in larger metropolises, and did not detract in any way from pride in the lines and growth of the city.

Eventually, of course, state highways crossing Macon County were developed. At first, they were dirt roads, but in a program that progressed slowly, the heavier traveled ones were first graveled and then oiled. Concrete and asphalt paving came with the use of motor vehicles, and got its heaviest start in the 1920s.

At some point, streets in Decatur also began to be improved. There is little information available on the sequence in which this was done, but an old newspaper account mentions the west entrance to town on Grand Avenue was one of the first. It can probably be assumed that the streets on which the stages traveled would have been others that were improved early. These would have included either South Main or South Franklin for the Shelbyville coach, North Main for the Bloomington coach, and William Street for the route that went by way of the Spangler Bridge to Bement and Monticello. Others would logically have been the four Main streets that radiated out from the square, other streets downtown, and the route to the depot after the railroads came. By 1910, there were 35 miles of paved streets in Decatur with more being paved as fast as the material could be secured and the work done.

In the early 1900s, Decatur was on the first interstate highway, the P.P.O.O. (the Pike's Peak Ocean-to-Ocean Highway) which passed through 14 states, serving more than 500 cities and villages, but was neglected when the modern network of interstate routes was authorized by Congress in 1956. That system left out Decatur to such an extent that it was the most left out of any city of its industrial importance in the United States. It was only in 1968 when Congress added 1,500 miles to the original 41,000 mile interstate system that a route was authorized for Decatur. Decatur is still being connected to other parts of the state by ongoing projects of building four-lane highways and interstates with exchanges here.

Drawn by Oxen

More and more settlers were then coming to this section of Illinois overland by wagons, which were sometimes drawn by oxen, sometimes by horses. Roads were being established, and "established" is about the kindest thing that one could truthfully say about them. Nor were they definitely or permanently "established." Black prairie soil was no better road material *than now, while there was then no drainage. On the prairie it was no trouble for any teamster to change the location of a road to avoid sloughs or quagmires and the new track which he made became the road.* [E. B. Hitchcock, Story of Decatur]

Railroads

As the wheels of a steam engine slowly begin to turn and gather speed, so did the growth of the city of Decatur with the coming of the railroad on April 21, 1854. Excited throngs gathered to greet the arrival of the first train to reach the city. The Illinois Central Railroad and the Great Western were in competition with each other to see which would get to Decatur first. The Great Western won the race. Illinois Central did not arrive until October 18, 1854, creating the first railroad intersection in the state of Illinois. Both railroads shared Union Station until 1903 when separate stations were built.

Thus began Decatur's long association with the rails. The Great Western changed names several times through mergers, and reorganized as the Wabash Railroad Company in 1889.

This "Follow the Flag" railroad served the midwest and heartland of America until the early 1960s. In 1964, the Wabash was absorbed by the Norfolk and Western Railroad. Nostalgia for those early years remains. The *Blue Bird*, the *Banner Blue* and the *Wabash Cannon Ball* are familiar names of trains that made regular runs through Decatur.

This is a 1926 photo of Joseph Swantz. He was a Wabash roundhouse employee who had more than 50 years of continuous service when he retired in 1927. In the 1860s it was reported that on Saturday paydays the Irish railroad workers raided the German labor camps and the Germans, with shovels, picks and clubs, retaliated.

> ### *Before the Railroads*
>
> *For a quarter of a century, from 1829, when the county was first organized, to 1854, when the first two railroads came, Macon county struggled against its paralyzing transportation handicap. Money was practically non-existent in as rich an agricultural region as the sun ever shone upon. There was no incentive for farmers to produce more than they could consume themselves because they could not sell a surplus. Their smiling acres could feed them, produce some of the raw material with which to clothe themselves and fuel to warm them, but that was all.* [E.T. Coleman, History of Macon County]

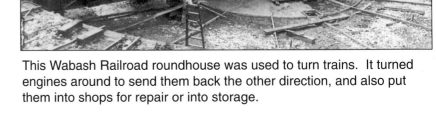

This Wabash Railroad roundhouse was used to turn trains. It turned engines around to send them back the other direction, and also put them into shops for repair or into storage.

An Aerial view the of Wabash Railroad shops and yards in May of 1954.

Wabash Railroad

The first Wabash roundhouse in Decatur was built in 1869 with eight stalls. In the 1870s oxen were used for switching cars in back of the Wabash and Illinois Central yards which were adjacent.

The Wabash Shops moved from Peoria to Decatur in 1884. A 42-stall roundhouse was raised in 1908, and at its peak the locomotive shops serviced 490 engines.

Decatur was the hub of the Wabash operations empire. In 1925 the railroad employed 3,500 Decatur workers. By 1965 the passenger car shops closed. When the Wabash merged with the Norfolk & Western in 1964, the number of Macon County residents on the Wabash payroll totaled 1,425.

Wabash Railroad steam engine #700 which was new in September of 1943. This series of steam engines was made in the Decatur shops.

The Wabash Railroad Class J, 4-6-2 steam engine #667 at the Decatur, Illinois engine shops on May 6, 1954. Classes A through I were assigned to locomotives owned by the Wabash Railroad in 1897. Classes indicated the wheel arrangements on the locomotives, and more classes were assigned in later years as the Wabash acquired locomotives with new wheel arrangements. The numbering system originated in 1856 with the first line, the Toledo, Wabash & Western. Even though the names of the lines changed over the years, the numbering system remained the same. As new power was added, the next higher available number was used.

The photo shows engine #573, the Wabash Railroad's last steam engine. Numbers 556-576 were first used in 1882 on new steam engines for the Wabash, St. Louis & Pacific.

The interior of a Wabash Railroad caboose on October 11, 1955. Cabooses were once used as a place for the crew to sleep and eat. Crew members also watched the train from the caboose, looking for signs of trouble on a curve, as well as making sure the train had cleared a crossing if it had to stop.

Below: The Wabash Railroad freight station and water tank near the Illinois Central crossing at Decatur on November 30, 1936. Water was a necessity to keep the steam engines running. A point of interest from *A Browser's Dictionary:* "When early steam engines ran dry at a town without a water tower, the crew had to 'jerk' water in buckets from wells and haul it to the locomotive. Hence, they contemptuously labeled the place a 'jerkwater town'."

The Illinois Terminal Railroad had its beginnings as Illinois Traction, an electric system operating through central Illinois and to St. Louis. Illinois Terminal Railroad officials from throughout central Illinois appear poised and professional in this 1908 photo. Back Row (left to right): R. McCalman, W.H. Burke, J.P. Doan, M.L. Burry, J.J. Tremper, L.E. Fischer. Middle row: M.G. Linn, B.E. Bramble, J.E. Johnson, C.F. Handshy, George M. Mattis. Front row: W.L. Murphy, A.C. Murray, H.C. Hoagland, Ed Bell, J.M. Bosenbury, J.P. Glover, H.J. Pepper. B.R. Stephens, the company's general traffic manager, stands in front and center.

A Wabash Railroad wreck at the St. Louis Bridge in Decatur on December 4, 1912. The worst Wabash fatality, however, occurred on July 19, 1974, when a tank car blew up in the railroad yards. The explosion killed seven employees and injured 300.

A Wabash Railroad class J-1, 4-6-2 steam engine #660 undergoing salvage operations on February 6, 1953. This picture shows the inside of the boiler. Wood and coal were burned to feed the boiler that ran the big steam engines.

An aerial view of the Wabash Railroad centennial in Decatur on May 16, 1954, near the engine shops. Included are F-7A's, 1188 and 1188A trains. Between 1885 and 1887 all engines had 1000 added to their numbers.

The Wabash Railroad EMD Model
E-7A diesel #1000 at Oakland
Avenue on August 19, 1946.

The *Bluebird* dome car, Wabash
Railroad. So very many Decatur residents have fond memories of riding on
this train, pictured in July of 1952.

The rear view of Illinois Terminal Railroad's
City of Decatur, one of the company's
streamlined electric trains, photographed
on October 21, 1948.

Illinois Central

The second railroad to bring service to Decatur was the Illinois Central on October 18, 1854. The bill to authorize a land grant of two and a half million acres to build the railroad was pushed through the Senate by Stephen A. Douglas and in the House by Abraham Lincoln and was signed by President Fillmore in 1850.

In 1907 at the peak of rail travel, 72 trains a day stopped in Decatur: 40 of which were operated by the Illinois Central and 25 by the Wabash.

The Illinois Central Railroad passenger train, the *Green Diamond,* draws a crowd of patrons on May 4, 1936.

The Illinois Central Railroad ticket office at 121 East William Street. This was also the ticket office for the Peoria, Decatur and Evansville Railroad (which used the Union Depot). The photo was taken on October 26, 1898, at the time of the first Corn Carnival in Decatur, which explains the interesting decorations.

The Corn Carnival, a gala event between 1895 and 1902, featured a corn palace made with ten tons of corn, a daily balloon ascension and a corn shucking contest between the mayor and the sheriff. Local businesses took on the appearance of haymows and corncribs.

Issued by the
NORFOLK AND WESTERN
RAILWAY COMPANY.
NON-TRANSFERABLE
LOCAL ONE WAY TICKET
SOLD SUBJECT TO TARIFF REGULATIONS.

FARE	TAX	TOTAL
$ 1 50	$ —	$ 1 50

EXPIRATION OF TICKET SHOWN BY PUNCH

Six months in addition to date of Sale........ ★

One Year in addition to date of Sale......... ★

OR .... ★

GOOD FOR ONE PASSAGE IN COACHES
UNLESS PUNCHED FIRST-CLASS - (Charge for Space Extra)

78498

R.H. Hubbard
General Passenger Sales Manager
Roanoke, Va. 24011

FORM L.-O.W.

First Class	★
Half Fare	★
Baggage	★

From..... TAYLORVILLE, ILL.

To..... DECATUR, ILL.

Endorsements

A Norfolk &Western Railway ticket for a trip from Taylorville to Decatur. The Wabash had merged with the N & W in 1964.

a la carte

SOUPS
Clam Chowder, Split Pea, Bean, Beef Noodle, Cream of Tomato, Chicken Noodle, Vegetable, Cream of Mushroom, Genuine Turtle (includes crackers or bread) .25

CEREALS
Toasted Corn Flakes, Grape Nuts, All-Bran, Shredded Wheat, Puffed Wheat or Rice (with cream) .25

RELISHES, APPETIZERS
Queen Olives .20   Tomato Juice .15   Orange Juice .15

MEATS
Choice Steak 1.35   Choice Loin Pork Chops (2) .95
Bacon or Ham and One Egg .75   Bacon or Ham and 2 Eggs .85
Egg, any style (1) .20   Eggs, any style (2) .35
Eggs, any style (3) .45

SANDWICHES
Fried Ham .45   Cold Meat .30
Cheese .30   Combination .45

BREAD
White, Whole Wheat, Rye (with butter) .10   Toast (buttered) .15

HOT DISHES
Chili Con Carne (includes crackers or bread) .30
Baked Beans, Hot or Cold .25   Spaghetti .25

FRIDAY SUGGESTIONS
Egg Salad Sandwich .30
Flaky Tuna Salad (Served with Potato Chips) .65

SALADS
Head Lettuce with Dressing .30   Sliced Tomatoes (in season) .30

VEGETABLES
French Fried Potatoes .20   Cottage Fried Potatoes .20

DESSERTS
Pie, liberal cut .20   Pie, liberal cut with cheese .30
Cake .20   Sliced Bananas with cream .25
Ice Cream .25

COFFEE, TEA, MILK
Coffee (cup) .10   Coffee (pot) .20   Tea (pot) .20
Milk (half-pint bottle) .15   Iced Tea .10

TO OUR PATRONS - - -
Thank you—The Illinois Terminal appreciates your patronage, and we trust it will be our privilege to serve you often.
The above prices include Illinois Retailers' Occupation Tax.

A menu from the *City of Decatur* Illinois Terminal Railroad car in 1949. An increase in rail traffic characterized the World War II years because of gasoline and rubber shortages.

Illinois Terminal Railroad logo.

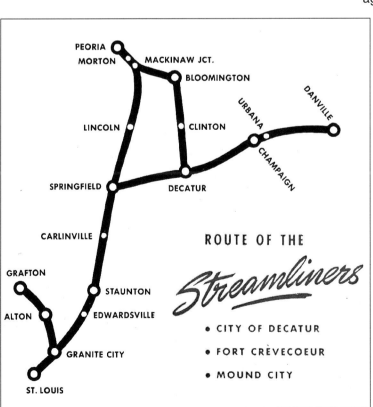

ROUTE OF THE

Streamliners

- CITY OF DECATUR
- FORT CRÈVECOEUR
- MOUND CITY

Map featuring the route of the Illinois Terminal Railroad Streamliners. In 1955 the last passenger car pulled out of Decatur for Champaign and Danville.

Interurban

In addition to the iron rails, at the turn of the century Decatur became part of the electric railway system that had its beginnings in Danville, Illinois. The Illinois Traction System, which later became known as the Illinois Terminal Railroad, began operations in 1901. Parlor cars and sleeping cars were a unique part of this interurban system. And Decatur again became the site of a railroad shop. All interior and exterior repairs could be made here as well as the construction of new cars and locomotives. The Illinois Terminal Railroad was one of the largest interurban systems in America. The *City of Decatur* began a Decatur-Springfield-St. Louis run on November 7, 1948. Freight service gradually overtook and replaced passenger service on the Interurban. The system was phased out in 1958 and with it a tradition and way of life came to an end. Gone were the arch-windowed cars, small town stops, the friendly crewmen and a piece of Americana.

In the 1880s electricity was being applied to street lighting but it had not yet reached the streetcar system. As seen here, mule power was still used by Decatur's two streetcar lines. However, they stayed remarkably well on schedule.

The East Illinois Power and Light Company car barn located at 436 East North Street. As the name indicates, it was a storage facility for the streetcars.

An Illinois Power and Light Company streetcar in front of the Wabash Railroad Depot.

The interior of a parlor car on the Illinois Traction System. Three such cars were put into operation in 1906. They were called buffet cars and meals were served on board. The cars were described as "the most elaborate cars ever constructed for regular service on an electric railway."

An Illinois Traction System parlor car, one of the *Corn Belt Limited* trains waiting with the conductor at the 100 block of North Main Street. The *Indiana* had stained glass at the top of its arched windows and gold leaf scrolling. No expense was spared to provide for the comfort of those traveling on the ITS. In 1930 the parlor cars were renovated and air conditioning was installed. The stained glass and arched windows were paneled over.

The interior of the main shop of the Illinois Traction System in 1910. The repair work on the cars was done in the various shops.

In 1909 the Traction System built car shops at 1800 East Garfield Avenue at a cost of $100,000. The Illinois Traction System became the Illinois Terminal Railroad in 1928. At this time passenger service, in competition with the personal automobile, declined. The shops' buildings were purchased in January 1956 by Parke Properties, Inc. for use as a warehouse.

The wood mill shop of the Illinois Traction System in 1910 worked on the railroad cars which, during that era, were made from wood. The ITS ran 500 miles of track.

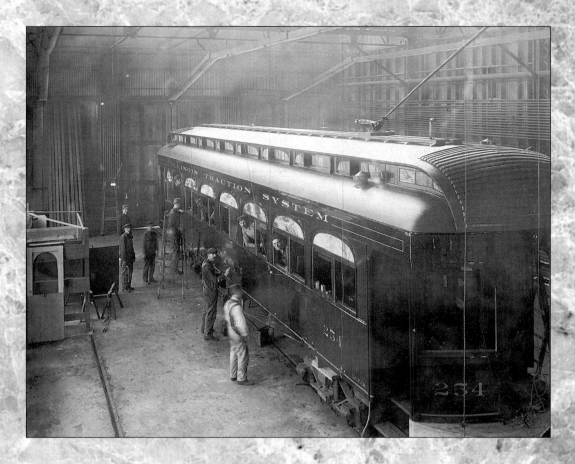

Workers at the Illinois Traction System paint shop in 1910. New cars were constructed for the Interurban in the Decatur shop. After World War II freight service surpassed passenger service as the moneymaker.

An Illinois Traction System line car used to check track, replace faulty wiring, and set poles for new wiring. Line repair became a real problem during the winter months when sleet caused wires to break. In order to repair the wire, the line car had to be able to use the 650-volt DC line to get to it. Thus, crews worked with live wires while doing repairs.

Bridges of Decatur

Water Transportation

Water transportation seemed to the pioneer the solution to the isolation of Illinois. It was natural that the settlers of Macon county should turn to the little Sangamon river as their particular outlet. They hoped to see this river made navigable in fact, as it was in law. The shallow draft flat-boat was to be the vehicle. This little river was navigable in spots at an ordinary stage of water. But there were many drifts, shoals, milldams and crooks which could not be successfully navigated except in very high water. We know that it was a plan to take a flat boat down the Sangamon river that led Abraham Lincoln into a contract with Denton Offutt which took him away from Macon county and to New Salem in Sangamon county. And, he ultimately accomplished it at cost of great labor and the overcoming of many difficulties. Young Lincoln was an experienced flatboat man, but he never made a second attempt. [E. B. Hitchcock, Story of Decatur]

This covered wooden bridge was the first bridge to be built across the Sangamon River. It was built in 1840 at the same site as the first ferry, and also served the Decatur-Shelbyville traffic. It was in use until being replaced in 1913 by a steel girder, illuminated bridge eight feet higher than the old one. When the Lake Decatur dam was built in 1921-23, that bridge had to be raised another 15 feet. It still serves traffic traveling southbound across the lake on Route 51. Northbound traffic travels across a new bridge opened in 1962.

Bridge traffic near the St. Louis railroad bridge on Route 48 in Decatur, built at the southwest edge of Decatur, 440 feet long, in 1925 and widened in 1957.

The Faries Park Bridge, a Wabash Railroad bridge, was built across the Sangamon River in 1907. At a cost of $200,000, the impressive structure was said to have been one of the biggest concrete jobs in the world.

The Wabash Railroad St. Louis Bridge on August 28, 1898 When the first train, the *Frontier*, chugged into town with it came opportunity and prosperity. Grain farmers and livestock owners could raise produce for outside markets. Industries could start, assured of markets for their goods. Expanded business and agriculture led to increased population.

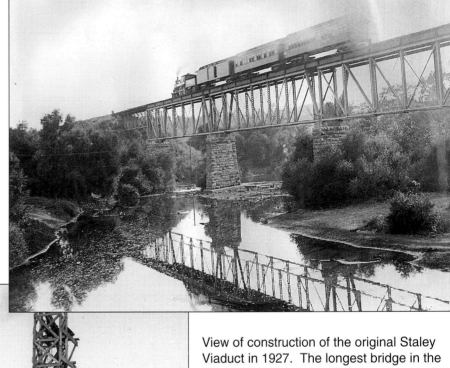

View of construction of the original Staley Viaduct in 1927. The longest bridge in the county did not carry traffic over water, but was built over the railroad yards. The first one was erected in 1927-28, and was 2,360 feet long. In May 1988, construction was begun on a new viaduct. On Friday, October 16, 1992, after many time and cost overruns, the viaduct was reopened. For the first time it had a formal name, the William B. Sands Viaduct, named for the city's director of public works. The bridge was four lanes wide instead of two, and, having been both widened and shortened, was now 1,900 feet long.

29

Transfer House

Decatur resident, Rex Cochran, had the good fortune of having a private audience with Pope Pius XII in Rome during World War II. Inquiring after the young serviceman's hometown Rex answered "Decatur, Illinois." The Pope exclaimed, "the little round house." He had driven through Decatur in the 1920s and well remembered the distinctive structure that one drove around in the center of town.

The Transfer House was a unique Decatur facility and almost an institution. Used as a transfer point for passengers continuing on to other destinations, the charming house also served as a retreat from the weather.

Moreover, it was a celebration stand. Some remember that when news of Japan's surrender on V-J Day, August 14, 1945, was announced, joyous passengers, hanging onto running boards, circled the Transfer House. Not to mention girls in shorts (banned by Police Chief Schepper's famous edict) who danced on top of the Transfer House. No one intervened.

Picture of the first Transfer House in use. Erected by the City Electric Railway Company, it was a rectangular structure 18 by 20 feet, stuccoed outside and plastered inside, heated by a stove. In 1895, merchants and property owners around the square raised enough money for a new Transfer House to be built to beautify the square. The old building was sold to John F. Mattes of Decatur Brick Manufacturing Company and was used as a company office at the end of East Wood Street in what is now Nelson Park. It was then sold to Frank R. Hahn of the Cement Products Company which operated at that location. The structure was later turned into a house for the Nelson Park Golf Course caddies off Route 36 East.

Raised in 1896, the new Transfer House dominates the square. A special car heads to the baseball game. This Transfer House was moved from Lincoln Square to Central Park in 1962 where it served various purposes until the Downtown Decatur Council established offices there in 1970.

The Transfer House of Yesteryear

Stage stands (transfer from one stage to another) were as necessary to highway traffic in those days as filling stations are today and their functions were analogous to those of the filling stations, although the two were not precisely identical. The stage stand was more than a filling station. It was a tavern where creature comforts were to be had for man and beast, but it was often a relay station, where stage horses were changed.

Today, if we choose to ignore the three perfectly good railroads to Springfield, it is a matter of an hour's drive by highway from one city to the other. It was then perhaps a two day's trip, or possibly longer. When roads were dry it could be made by a stage with its relays of horses, but private vehicles could not take advantage of relays. These stage stands were scattered along all stage roads and private homes made shift to accommodate travelers in a pinch. [E.T. Coleman]

This is a view looking north on Main Street toward the Transfer House on June 23, 1938. Fred MacMurray was starring in *Coconut Grove* at the Lincoln Theater.

Bus patrons waiting at the Transfer House in October of 1937.

The entryway of the Transfer House showing the thermometer on March 18, 1940.

31

The Horse at Work

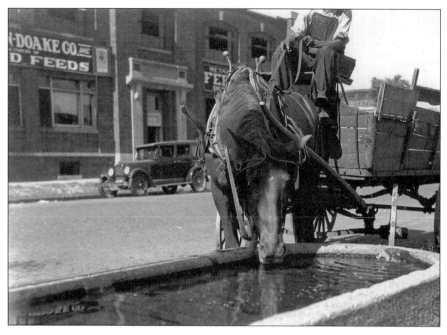

Horseback and afoot were the earliest modes of travel when Macon County was first settled in 1829. Sometimes in the spring when the trails were bottomless mud, both horse and rider sunk deep. Those early traces and Indian trails became stage routes before the advent of the railroad. Warnick's Tavern, south of the Sangamon River, was the first stage stop where man and beast could stop overnight. The next stage stand in 1840, Miller's Tavern, north side of U.S. Route 36, had a horse barn that accommodated 22 horses. Stage coaches were pulled by four horses. The U.S. Mail came into Decatur by horseback. Silas Packard, the mail carrier, said that besides wild deer, his horse was his only companion on his Decatur to Bloomington two-day trips.

On a hot July day in 1933, the only public drinking trough left for horses in the city was in the 400 block of East Main Street. Here Old Dobbin is necking to allay the thirst which the sun's rays have created.

A turn-of-the-century Davis Livery Company wagon delivering *Decatur Review* newspapers.

The Byrd L. Davis, Sr. Livery Stable in 1911. The first Davis stable was located at 564 North Water Street and was followed by others in the 100 block of East Cerro Gordo, at Franklin and Park streets, and one on South Main. At the height of his business, Davis employed 35 men and had 40 horses for hire. As time went on, he replaced his horses with trucks and went into the storage transfer business.

A Meadow Gold horse-drawn milk wagon still in use on August 24, 1947.

Different modes of transportation co-existed, sharing the same roads in Decatur in March 1930.

Street Work

Brick paving of West Decatur Street near Fairview Avenue. Decatur's first hard-surface street was laid in 1884 when brick with sand filler was put on Lincoln Square.

Photo right: Paving West Main Street from Church Street. Riding the streetcars was the only way one could travel out West Main Street from Church Street in November 1913, when this picture was taken. After tracks were laid on a concrete base, the street was paved with creosoted blocks, but not before there was a long argument on the merits of the blocks as opposed to brick. Those supporting creosoted blocks pointed out they were noiseless, easier to clean, and more durable than brick. From 1915 to 1919, many streets were paved with the blocks. A total of 3.6 miles of wood block pavement was laid, with the blocks placed on a six-inch concrete base. The blocks were creosoted to prevent absorption of moisture. Within a few years, it became apparent that the creosote deteriorated to the extent that the blocks swelled with moisture causing bumps to form making travel over them difficult. The side pressure from blocks laid between streetcar tracks would shove the rails out of line so badly that sometimes cars were derailed. Heavy rains caused street flooding that actually floated away the loosened blocks. The tar with which the blocks were creosoted oozed to the surface on warm days causing public disillusionment with this form of pavement. The blocks were gradually removed and given away as fireplace fuel. Most were removed between 1925 and 1934, but the last were not taken up

until 1954 on South Water between Washington and Wood.

In recent years, paving in Decatur has been done with concrete and asphalt. Since 1970, street resurfacing has been done largely under a new process whereby the surface of the old pavement is scarified by a machine that mixes new asphalt with old material loosened by the scarifying, producing a new surface from both the old and new material. This method costs about half as much as traditional techniques for resurfacing.

The Illinois Traction System subway at Harrison Avenue under construction in 1910. The subway was built to take street traffic under the tracks.

This photo, looking north toward East Prairie, shows street sweepers at work on Merchant Street in May 1910.

There was little mechanical equipment in road repair work before 1911. This worker was grading East Wood Street with horse power in August of that year. In earlier days when a road needed to be repaired those living on the road turned up to fix it. It was like a barn raising social affair with everyone having a great time except those who needed to use the road to get through.

A double contest was held in Clinton in 1911. The first was motor vs. horse in the "fast and efficient road work" category. The horse lost. "A flaunting defiance flung at the citadel of Old Dobbin." The other was true competition: motor vs motor—different types of new gas engines (not steam) going head to head or engine to engine; such as the Fairbanks Morse against the Aultman Taylor (photo). A kind of Indy 500 of early tractors. At any rate the result was that by 1912, more equipment had been adapted to use for Decatur street and road work.

Main Street

The 300 block of North Main Street looking north and east from the intersection at William Street. Notice the varied forms of transportation in use in 1910—horse and buggy, "horseless carriage," bicycle and streetcar.

Looking east toward Franklin Street at South Park Street in 1927.

Gas Stations

As the automobile age descended on Decatur the early vehicles demanded constant repair, and of equal importance, fuel. The very early owners were their own mechanics. In all kinds of weather they were required to change poor quality tires on even poorer quality roads. Early fuel stations were part of repair shops or dealerships and very service oriented. Hence, the days when the driver pulled into a gas station and two attendants appeared instantaneously, not only to fill the tank, but wash windows, check oil and tires. Those were the days!

Many remember the Texaco Station at 486 North 22nd Street by the Staley Viaduct in 1953.

Texaco Station owners and employees. From left, owner Rex Cochran, Delmar Thompson, owner Harold Carter and Harold Roberts took a photograph break in May 1953.

The Spur Oil Station at 756 North Main Street on July 1, 1949. Spur Distributing also owned a station in the 600 block of East Wood street with Peter Oreskovich serving as general manager for both locations. Originally gas stations resembled houses or residences. By the '50s they took on a more box-like or streamlined appearance with several stalls to accommodate cars and car hoists.

Photo below: New buses ready for service. Ten buses doubled Decatur's transportation system in December 1936. Six of the ten came from the Illinois Power and Light Corporation (I. P. & L.). Between 40 and 50 employees of I.P. & L. were taken over by the Decatur City Lines which also purchased the I.P. & L. bus garage. The new buses were valued at $6,000 each and were built by General Motors in Pontiac, Michigan. A five-cent fare was charged to the riding public plus a one-cent charge for transfers. Schoolchildren's tokens cost four cents.

A bus and train at the West Main and Oakland streets intersection before the subway was built in 1936. The Millikin University campus is visible in the background.

Photo below: Early Decatur aviators, the Hunter brothers, circa 1918.

The first sustaining flight made in Illinois was in Decatur on July 14, 1910. At the Downing racetrack, later to become Hess Park. A sustaining flight meant that it covered a few miles rather than up and down in the same field as had occurred in Chicago in 1909. The Decatur pilot was Charles Willard, a pioneer in aviation. The first airport was built on Route 36, three miles west of Decatur on land leased by John H. Kiick, a wealthy retired farmer. The name of the plane is *Big Blue*, no doubt the plane carried fans or employees of Millikin University.

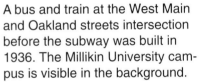

Made in Decatur

Decatur has boasted a long line of inventors who did their share toward the revolution of the industrial world. Many of their discoveries are still manufactured here and are leaders in their class. There were John Beall, the Haworths, Hieronymus Mueller, Robert Faries, W. H. Bramble, A. W. Cash, Caleb Smith, Curtis King and numerous others. Decatur was the beginning of the power corn sheller, much valuable milling machinery, the checkrower, an automatic machine for making checkrower wire, a water-tapping machine, wire mate streetcar trucks, valves for submarines, locks for post office boxes, fly-swatters, automatic grain weighers. And the list goes on.

The street striper, an invention of H. L. Lewis of Decatur, was in use on July 13, 1936.

The pencil sharpener was invented by Mrs. Bertha Gray Storer of Decatur.

The Comet automobile was made in Decatur in the 1920s. Parts were brought in from outside the city, and small castings came from Decatur Malleable Iron Works. Comet did the upholstery work and installed tops and window curtains. At its peak, Comet made less than 2,000 cars a year; their output was never above six cars a day. The company was part of a World War I boom, but when a recession hit the auto industry, contracts and orders did not come in as expected, and the company passed into receivership in 1923.

In 1828, Captain David L. Allen drove into Decatur in the finest carriage the town had ever seen. Allen had $1,600 cash in his pocket and a land grant for 160 acres. He immediately purchased an additional 80 acres and involved himself in several businesses including a grist and sawmill on the Sangamon River. On the opposite bank, Allen established Decatur's first industry—a lime kiln.

Industrial growth in the young city was born of necessity. The first real surge in Decatur's population growth came in 1870. The Decatur Rolling Mill moved to the city to produce the iron rails needed for railroad expansion. Employees were hired and brought in to work the mill. A citywide water system was installed to meet the needs of the mill and the city. This population surge created a need for businesses and industries to provide the products for the comfort and well being of Decatur's citizenry. Roads were paved, brick makers came in, garment factories were established, and coal was discovered to fuel it all.

Decatur was a natural as a grain processing cen-

The Spencer-Kellogg plant shown on December 8, 1939.

ter. A number of the implements used to plant and harvest the grain were invented locally. An impressive number of inventions and improvements to existing products came out of Decatur. Known as a "blue collar" town, the city has been highly dependent on heavy industry for its economic success since the early days.

The industrial boom slowed after World War II, and today's growth comes not from heavy industry but in the areas of retail and service. Those early settlers who speculated that the city's development would go south of the Sangamon River would be very surprised at the recent spurt of growth on Decatur's far north side. Just as the city stretched out along the transportation centers—i.e. the railroads—after the 1850s, today's growth is occurring around Decatur's main transportation arteries—Interstate 72 and Highway 51.

Lyon Lumber

Joseph Mills (left) was a Decatur lumberman who bought land at the corner of North Main and William streets in 1853 and started a carpentry shop. Between 1853 and 1878, he erected the First Methodist Church, Stapp's Chapel, D. S. Shellabarger house and the James Millikin house. In 1878 he became a partner of W. B. Hary in a lumber business. In 1911 the Mills Lumber Company was sold to the Lyon Company.

Shown above is the interior of the Lyon Lumber Company at 546 East Cerro Gordo Street.

Early Woodworker

E. O. Smith was charged for the making of five plain panel doors at the rate of $4.50 each. This was in November, 1839. It will be remembered that these doors were made by hand, probably out of rough native lumber. It takes a skilled mechanic to make a plain panel door, and it is an interesting matter for speculations as to the cost of making them in the same way today.

From an account with one George Daly it appears that Mr. Dillehunt made a coffin for a small child for which he charged $2, and a plain dining table for $5. He received in pay one and a half bushels of wheat at 50 cents a bushel, eight pounds of bacon ham at 4 cents a pound, four chickens at 6 1/4 cents a piece, twenty-six pounds of pork at 2 cents a pound and forty pounds of the same at the same price. [E.T. Coleman]

A view of the exterior of the Lyon Lumber Company on January 15, 1954. The firm operated for almost 100 years, primarily engaged in millwork.

A 1905 photograph of the Mueller family. Mueller had come to America at age 17 and died in Decatur at age 68. His six sons carried on operations of the expanding North American firm.

The family sold its interest in 1987. Currently Mueller Company forms part of Tyco International Limited, a publicly held corporation based in Exeter, New Hampshire.

The Mueller Company Band in 1913 (with mascot) provided unlimited lighthearted music and entertainment for company and city picnics, outings and Fourth of July celebrations.

Mueller Company baseball team fans, seated on bleachers, root for their co-workers and family members in this turn-of-the-century photo.

Chambers, Bering & Quinlan

William B. Chambers and William J. Quinlan began their business in 1872. Mr. James E. Bering joined the partnership in 1876, and stock was issued in 1882. According to the City of Decatur's 1887-88 Manufacturing and Mercantile Resources guide, C B & Q manufactured many labor saving devices. Some of those devices included the "hawkeye" hay loader, the U.S. combined checkrow corn planter, the C B & Q corn planter with covering blades, the C B & Q reversible carrier, the hawkeye fork to unload hay, the Brown hog ringer as well as the Champion hog ringer.

From 1850 to 1900 Decatur was home to many farm implement makers. Haworth & Son, founded in 1861, first manufactured the world-renowned checkrow corn planter, an invention of George Haworth to guarantee straight rows for corn planters. In one of its first years, 16,000 sold in the nation.

This Chambers, Bering & Quinlan Company office building was erected in 1861 for Barber & Hawley, manufacturers of farm implements. About 1872 it became known as Decatur Agricultural Works, then as Chambers, Bering & Quinlan. Located at 662 North Jasper, the facility was torn down in October 1906.

Three women at work for C B & Q during the war years. This photo was taken on April 26, 1943.

At work at CB&Q in July 1943. In 1979 Wagner Castings Company absorbed C B & Q, three years short of the company's centennial.

General Electric

General Electric maintained a plant in Decatur from 1947 until 1975. Located in the Victory Military Engine Company complex on North 22nd Street, the plant was the chemical and plastics unit of General Electric. Audio product expansion in 1960 led to the establishment of a record-changer plant in the 900 block of East Locust Street. When the plants closed down, the city lost a combined total of over 600 jobs. The reason given for closing the plants was foreign competition.

Step one in construction of a G.E. audio unit was the inspection of the cabinets. Though not made in Decatur, the cabinets were made to G.E.'s specifications and thoroughly inspected on arrival at the local plant. The cabinets were then sent to the line where components were added to the shells. The final product was tested, inspected and ran through quality checks. Products of the Decatur plant included electric guitars, portable phonograph combinations, monaural and stereo portable hi-fi phonographs, portable and console phonographs with AM/FM stereo radios, portable and stereo tape recorders and TV phonograph combinations.

Women working in the General Electric plastics plant on December 29, 1949. G.E. phased out its plastics division in 1960. It had occupied the North 22nd Street location since shortly after the end of World War II.

Marvel-Schebler

The Marvel-Schebler-Tillotson division of Borg-Warner Corporation came to Decatur in 1948. The plant produced carburetors, ignition components and emission controls for the automotive industry. In 1958 York division of the firm came to assemble Ford-o-matic transmissions, auto air conditioners and components. In 1982 the Marvel-Schebler-Tillotson division was phased out, leaving the York division, which employed about 450 workers.

In the 1950s the manufacturer became involved in the production of nuclear power control devices and a three-story lab was raised. Admiral H. Rickover came to Decatur to check on the progress in parts to be used in the navy's submarines.

Man at work at Marvel-Schebler plant in 1950.

Aerial view of Borg-Warner (Marvel-Schebler) in February of 1959.

Small parts machining at Marvel-Schebler in November of 1950.

Iron Works

Leader began business in Decatur in 1888 as a brick manufacturer. In 1905, the firm switched to making water pressure systems. Adapting to trends of the time, Leader shifted gears in 1920 by manufacturing farm and bulk oil storage equipment. By 1930, the firm moved into custom manufacturing of food, chemical and petroleum processing equipment. Leader became a division of Standard Steel in 1957. The company discontinued operations circa 1972. ADM currently uses the Leader facility, pictured above in 1905, as a warehouse.

Railroad Iron

From 1870 to 1880 were momentous years for Decatur. The city was expanding and taking on city ways. A real thrill came when in 1871 a rolling mill was established.

Here was a plant to turn out railroad iron in the midst of railroad activity. It employed from 300 to 500 skilled men. They were paid well. The plant east of the railroad station boomed the east part of the city. It was a real boom business. [E.T. Coleman]

A 1911 photo of Union Iron Works at 600-660 East William Street. Union Iron was established by James Millikin and C. C. Burroughs in 1864 to make engines. The main product was the Western Corn Sheller designed by John Beall, a millwright and grain elevator builder. Also produced at the foundry were steam engines and boilers. Union was the first Decatur industry to use electricity as a motive power and to buy it from a public utility. Union moved to Warrensburg in 1976. The company vacated its plant in 1981 and consolidated with Superior Welding at 900 East Division Street. In 1983 Superior was sold to Curry Equipment and Sales, Inc. of Oreana. Robert Curry, president, moved Union Iron back to Decatur at 1102 North 18th Street in 1983. The company still manufactures grain handling equipment and systems.

Wagner Castings Company

Wagner Castings Company had its beginnings in 1917 when A. W. Wagner made castings for a Peoria firm that was a predecessor to Caterpillar Tractor. The Wagner firm expanded extensively, and by the 1970s recorded a normal payroll at 1,800 workers. In 1979 Wagner absorbed one of Decatur's leading industries, Chambers Bering & Quinlan.

A.W.'s son, John A. Wagner, took up his duties as company timekeeper after honorable discharge from the U.S. Marines in 1919. He assumed the presidency of Wagner Castings Company on May 25, 1933.

In April 1983 a group of eight Wagner employees purchased the firm. This group, in turn, sold to an Ohio-based holding company, Sudbury, Inc. in 1987.

Currently 75% percent of Wagner's business comes from the automotive industry. Ford, Chrysler and GM are Wagner's three major customers to whom they supply automotive parts.

The company continues to operate under the Wagner name at 825 North Lower Street.

A. W. Wagner, Founder

John A. Wagner, Sr.
Industrialist and civic leader

Homes provided for Decatur Malleable Iron workers in 1916 (currently near Woodford Street). Some of these households were soon to lose the male providers as Congress was about to ratify the Selective Service Act.

A.W. Wagner served as the first president of Decatur Malleable Iron Company in 1916 with Donald E. Willard as vice president and Irving A. Staley, secretary-treasurer. The company, originally located at North Woodford and Curtis streets, moved to 751 North Lower by 1918.

Purchased by Illinois Malleable in 1936, the foundry closed in March of 1937 (photo above). The firm's final address was listed at 1530 East Curtis Street.

54

1943 was a productive transition year for the Wagner Company. 1,600,000 pounds of casting for war use came from the company foundry each month: 120 Wagner men were called to active duty and it was the year that Rosie the Riveter and her ilk entered a man's domain. At Wagner's 15 women worked in the foundry and 25 in the machine shop.

During peacetime malleable castings had been shipped to auto manufacturers. With America at war Wagner production increased by 50%. Pig iron, scrap and limestone translated into malleable iron used to manufacture parts and valves used on navy transports, destroyers, parts for gun mounts, armored cars and tanks. A fast working man averaged 200 molds a day. Each set and poured his own mold, carrying ladles which held 50 pounds of iron heated to 2,800 degrees Fahrenheit.

Working inside Wagner Casting Company in February 1984. By comparison with the above photo, work has become highly mechanized in the industry. Workers no longer catch and run with the iron but are stationary. A ladle, holding 500 pounds of iron, moves on a monorail and a conveyor transports the molten iron.

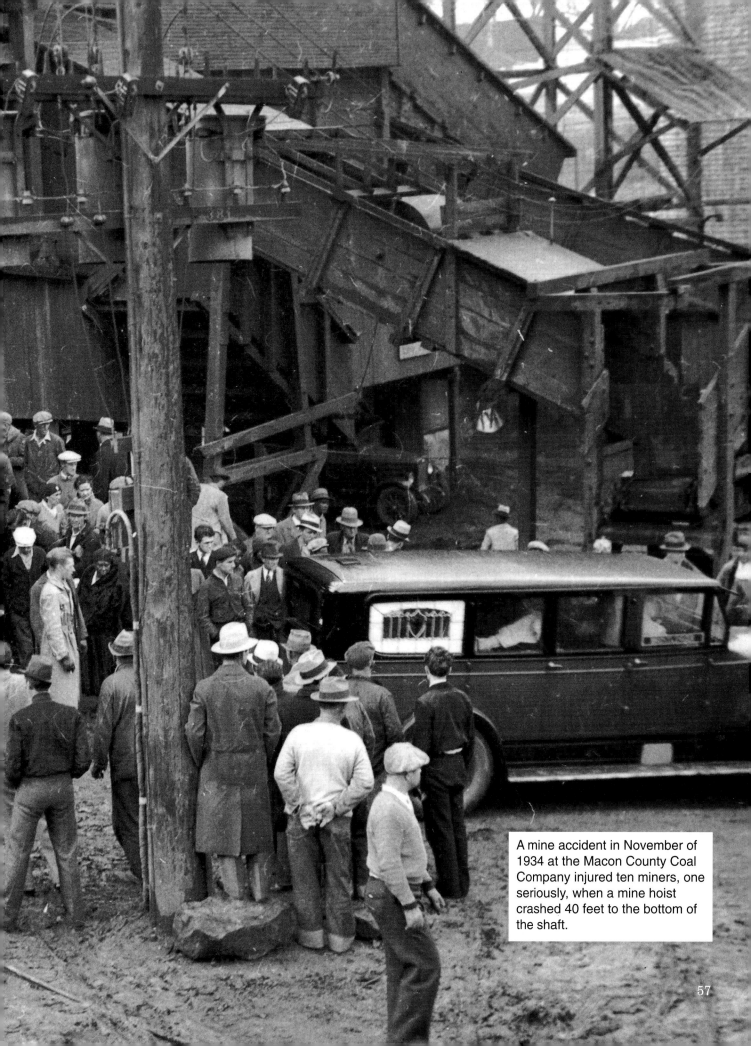

A mine accident in November of 1934 at the Macon County Coal Company injured ten miners, one seriously, when a mine hoist crashed 40 feet to the bottom of the shaft.

Coal Mining

J. W. Bering discovered a 290-foot coal shaft in the 1800 block of East Eldorado in 1880. Coal was mined there until 1885. Decatur Coal Company mined a shaft near Broadway (now Martin Luther King, Jr. Drive) and East Prairie until 1927. Decatur's largest produc-ing mine, Macon County Coal Company was sunk on South Main Street in 1903. The competing coal companies eventually consolidated operations under a single manager.

Ben Waggoner was a coal dealer in Decatur for 27 years before his death in 1939. The coal yard he operated is believed to be the oldest in Decatur, having been founded in 1887 by F.D. Caldwell and sold to Waggoner in 1912. Waggoner took in Joseph Michl as a partner in 1937 and sold his share of the business to Michl in 1939.

Gathering coal during the coal shortage in the winter of 1936.

Below: Coal mine salvage in February 1947 when Macon County Coal closed. The firm employed 450 miners during peak periods. It had mined a good vein at 360 feet.

Turned to Future

In 1890, The Review *published a trade and industrial supplement in which it was said:*

"It was ten years ago that Decatur turned her face to the future. Her citizens awoke to the possibilities that were before them. About this time the fuel problem was solved by an unlimited supply of as fine a quality of coal as can be found anywhere in the great coal state of Illinois. The railroad facilities were unequalled; the natural advantages all that could be asked for, and they wisely determined that by united and active effort on their part, Decatur might be made a great commercial and manufacturing center."

In the ten years from 1880 to 1890 the population had more than doubled. Business blocks were going up and manufactories of all kinds were started. [E.T. Coleman]

Miners meet at Nelson
Park in September 1932.

Mine Violence

Tension had been building between supporters of the Progressive Miners Association (PMA) on strike and the backers of the United Mine Workers of America (UMWA) who refused to strike in the fall of 1932.

The UMWA had been picketed by up to 500 members and supporters of the PMA.

Fifty deputies and policemen, armed with guns, tear gas and axe handles, under the orders of Sheriff E.C. Wilson, routed the picketing miners. More than 40 men and women were arrested. Police blamed the women in the "mob of 500" for inciting the crowd and refusing to disperse.

Miners charged that the move by authorities using force and tear gas was at the request of mine operators to discourage the strike.

Miners' homes were bombed during the violence of November 1932.

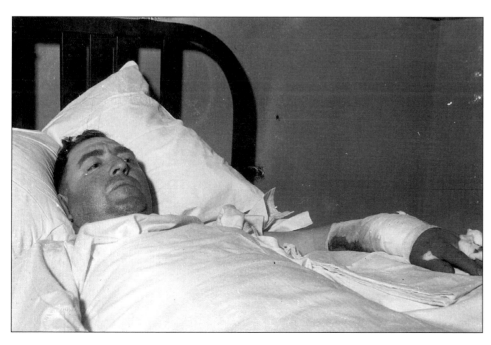

Pete Borgogne, at 872 South Franklin Street, was shot in the arm from behind as he was driven off, with other miners, before deputized national guardsmen. On November 4, 1932, when Sheriff E.C. Wilson set out to break up the picket line at the Macon County Coal Company. William Dennison, at 1251 Cottage Hill Avenue, was also shot in the head and wounded ten minutes later.

Caterpillar Inc.

Caterpillar chose Decatur for a plant when the company was expanding in the 1950s because of the company's good experience with a military engine plant here during World War II. Construction of the Decatur facility began in 1954 and the first motor grader rolled off the assembly line in June of 1955.

Today the Decatur facility is one of the major locations for the Mining & Construction Equipment Division of Caterpillar Inc. The Decatur facility: employs approximately 2,800, covers about 450 acres, includes more than 20 buildings, produces nine models of motor graders, eight models of off-highway trucks, and eleven models of wheel tractor-scrapers.

Caterpillar's commitment to serving the mining industry with a broad line of products led to the development of the 240-ton mining truck and the large wheel loader in Decatur in 1987. Since then, production of the largest mining truck has been incorporated into the Assembly Highway to meet expanding customer demands. The large wheel loader is now produced at MCE-Joliet.

Caterpillar has manufacturing facilities in 31 cities around the world, and dealers in nearly 130 countries.

This 908,000 square foot plant and office on a 426-acre site was the Caterpillar facility in Decatur in October of 1955 when wheel tractors first were produced here. The Decatur facility now is one of the main locations for the Mining & Construction Equipment Division of Caterpillar Inc. Motor graders, wheel tractor-scrapers and construction and mining trucks are manufactured here now.

Old Number 1, the first machine produced at the Decatur Plant, rolled off the line in June of 1955. One of its first jobs was this one at Syracuse University, Syracuse, New York. The well-travelled motor grader worked an estimated 17,000 hours and was returned to the Decatur facility for the 25th Anniversary Celebration in 1980. It now resides in an honored display in the Hall of Quality.

Combination Fountain

At one time, Decatur was known nationwide for manufacturing soda fountains.

Decatur businessman, Caleb Smith, is credited with making the first modern soda fountain in 1892.

Smith and his partner, Frank P. Howard, displayed their soda fountain in a showroom in the 700 block of North Water Street.

Smith later was associated with three soda fountain manufacturers in Decatur—Combination Fountain, Walrus Manufacturing Company and Decatur Fountain. By 1908 the three companies employed 350 to 400 men and produced 1,200 fountains a year.

One of Decatur's first soda fountains was operated by I. N. Irwin, a druggist. The first Coca Cola soft drink ever sold in Decatur was drawn by him in 1892.

Irwin also claimed the distinction of serving the first ice cream soda, a combination of ice cream, flavoring and soda water, in 1886.

The soda fountain, and the "soda jerk" who operated it, were a major part of American culture through the 1950s. Ice cream sodas, shakes, sundaes and bananas splits were as popular then as pizza is with today's youth.

Frank P. Howard (second from top), who died September 22, 1922, was president and one of the founders of the Combination Fountain and Decatur Brass Company. He invented and manufactured a type of fountain for confectionery stores. In this 1912 newspaper photograph he is shown with his father, J.S. Howard, his daughter Mrs. George Fuller and his granddaughter, who became Mrs. H.H. Myers.

Located at the corner of Morgan and Division streets, this building housed the Combination Fountain Company which was a pioneer in its field when it was founded in 1898.

Faries Manufacturing Company

Robert Faries, Decatur manufacturer, inventor, president of Faries Manufacturing and founder of the Walrus Manufacturing Company died on November 17, 1919. His inventions included a machine for making checkrower wire, revolving show window fixtures and the Autoposean attachment for cameras. In 1881 he founded Faries Manufacturing Company at 1060 East Grand where checkrower wire and home electric and gas fixtures were manufactured. In 1910 he bought Wilson Park and the name was changed to Faries Park, which many residents continue to enjoy today.

In 1909 Walrus Manufacturing took over a structure raised by Decatur Woolen Mills at 650 North Broadway. The specialty firm produced fixtures for schools, soda fountains and drug stores. Walrus goods were exported all over the world. Walrus maintained over 600 linear feet of floor space to showcase the company's products. The University of Illinois was a primary customer, purchasing equipment for its chemistry buildings and annex. Butcher blocks and refrigerators were the first items made by Walrus with soda fountains and fixtures added in 1903. The world's largest soda fountain, 88 feet in length with 44 seats, was assembled by Walrus in 1914 for a Texas soda shop. Walrus closed in March of 1972.

Pictured is Faries Manufacturing at 1036 East Grand in 1909. Manufacturer-inventor Robert Faries contributed one of the nation's most important farm inventions: after devising a wire machine in his basement workshop in 1873, he employed 65 workers at the Decatur Novelty Shop behind his house on Grand Avenue to make checkrow wire. In the later years of his life, Faries focused his considerable energies on nature study and photography.

Model Brass Company was a non-ferrous foundry originally located at 502-508 South Franklin when it opened in the 1920s. From the Chambers, Bering & Quinlan foundry and from the castings department of Model Brass came valves used on nearly every type of warship in the U.S. Navy. This photo from August of 1944 was taken at the company's 232-240 East Decatur site. The latter served as its home for 40 years until the structure was torn down in 1966 for the Greenwood Urban Renewal project. Model Brass listed in the City Directory in 1971 for the last time at 271 South 27th Street.

Decatur was early on a furniture manufacturing center. The Decatur Chair Factory (photo left) at 260 North Broadway was incorporated in 1905 with Charles J.F. Kraft named president.

This facility served as Caterpillar's Military Engine Company plant. After World War II it was taken over by the U.S. Army as the Decatur Signal Corps Depot and was phased out in 1962.

Firestone located its tire manufacturing plant in Decatur in 1963 due to the proximity of the Caterpillar Tractor Company plant. Firestone paid two million dollars for the site and within ten years the plant had a payroll of 2,000 employees and was turning out six million tires per year. This production level made it the fourth largest of all Firestone plants nationwide.

"The Cinderella Crop of the Century"

Crazy American

"Oh, that man?" said the moon-faced oriental. "He's the crazy American. For many months he has been here in North China, wandering through our fields from dawn to dusk. He pulls up soya plants and stares long at them."

Here he smiled and lowered his voice: "They say he was sent by his government. It is so amusing. The miracle bean has been a part of our life for ages. Suddenly it is discovered by Americans. Such queer people." [E.J. Dies on William Joseph Morse in 1907]

Tales could be told of early opposition to the two major soy products—meal and oil—in the present age. A.F. Staley fought in the early battles for a place for soybean products in the commercial arena.

In the soybean's struggle for recognition the true test came when the industry moved into mass production, with inherent merchandising challenges. Two companies, the A.E. Staley Manufacturing Company, began crushing in 1922, and the Archer Daniels Midland Company, in 1929—huge-scale producers with the expansion of the crop, followed by Central Soya Company, Inc., established in 1935.

Staley lived to see his operation rise to giant proportions and to see Decatur garner the title of Soybean Capital through enlargement of his own firm, of Archer Daniels Midland Company and of Spencer Kellogg and Sons, Inc. Decatur Soy Products Company also had a small plant at Decatur. Staley died on December 26, 1940 at the age of 73.

Gene Staley was a powerful factor in the industry's development. He was born and grew up in North Carolina. The story goes that at age seven, a missionary gave him a few seeds with instructions to plant them. He did, they grew and soy was added to the family diet.

Disliking farm life, young Gene Staley went on the road selling food products, including starch. By 1912, he had begun making his own starch from a corn plant in Decatur.

With investment capital of 1,500 dollars and his inherent genius, he built one of the largest corn refining businesses in the country. When he extolled the merits of the soybean, central Illinois farmers knew he believed it, and they were convinced. It was his years of background in merchandising corn-gluten feed that impressed buyers when later he pleaded the case of soybean oil meal as a part of their protein concentrate.

Six years before he began processing, Gene Staley had won the confidence of many farmers. Before launching his processing plant he had observed the experimental work of his predecessors. Illinois land had been "corned" to death during World War I.

Farmers were open to the soybean, but they needed an enlarged market. They had raised the plants for hay and forage and fertilizer, and could see no hope for the beans except as seed until processing developed.

In the eight years beginning in 1922, Staley and other early processors developed procedures that made maximum production possible. In those years, they improved the quality of soybean oil meal for animal nutrition in palatability and digestibility. The higher quality meal and oil helped lift returns to the farmer, and growing and processing of soybeans came into the range of economic competition with other deeply entrenched oil meals and oils.

In 1924, Staley experienced a setback. "This year other manufacturers entered the market and prices were bid up so high to secure enough soybeans to keep plants running that business showed a severe loss. Our loss for one month's operation amounted to approximately twelve thousand dollars."

The American Soybean Association started holding meetings. State departments of agriculture issued new literature, universities increased the work of experimenting with soy cultivation, farm machinery manufacturers and railroads added their efforts to the campaign for expansion. In 1925 Illinois, the heart of soy cultivation, threshed 1,431,000 bushels, in 1928 the total was 3,069,000 and in 1935 it rose to 24,012,000 bushels. By reason of educational work among the farmers the yields per acre increased in a decade from 13.5 bushels in 1925 to 18.0 in 1935. Meanwhile as the years passed new processing mills began to dot the soy belt.

Courtesy of *Herald & Review*

The Soybean

The humble soybean comes from a plant that produces pods containing tan beans about 1/4 inch in diameter. In 1982 when the *Kernel and the Bean* was published chronicling the history of the A.E. Staley Manufacturing Company, soybeans were the number one cash crop in the United States. The soybean plant packs a lot of protein, and soy products on the market and in development help feed the world's population. Its potential is virtually limitless.

Decatur Soy Products Plant at 518 Gault near St. James School in April of 1953. Archer Daniels Midland used this location as storage by 1964. It now lies abandoned. Tabor Grain was also another smaller similar firm on West Main.

Jasper DiGiovanna, president of Decatur Soy Products, a smaller enterprise than the local giant producers. This photo was taken on April 30, 1953. It was not uncommon for those of Italian extraction, formerly involved in the olive oil trade, to cross over to the soybean processing industry.

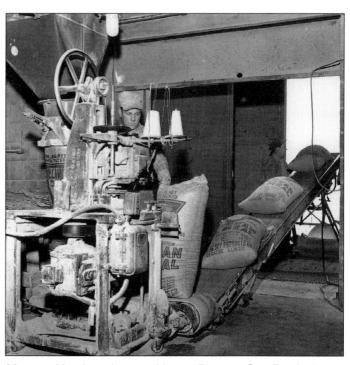

Man working bagging machine at Decatur Soy Products. The company was organized in 1940 and became Decatur Elevator Company in 1956, also run by DiGiovanna. It closed in the late '50s because of a low profit margin.

Spencer Kellogg

Spencer Kellogg and Sons, Inc. had stepped into the soybean industry in 1935 and by 1942 had plants in four cities, under the personal direction of Howard Kellogg, Jr. The firm came to Decatur from Buffalo, New York. The plant, purchased from W. L. Shellabarger, was located just north of the Wabash Railroad on Brush College Road (currently ADM West Plant). Soybean oil at that time was used in paint, linoleum, soaps and other products. The byproduct, bean meal, was used in livestock feed.

Man filling 100-pound Shellabarger bag with Soyflake flour at Spencer Kellogg on December 30, 1940. Spencer Kellogg bought out Shellabarger Grain Products in 1938, but W. L. Shellabarger remained in charge of soybean operations after the sale.

The Staley Company's spectacular success drew two major grain processors to Decatur: Spencer-Kellogg as well as Archer Daniels Midland. Geared for heavy soybean processing, the newly formed triumvirate earned Decatur her "world soybean capital" title. Pictured here is an aerial view of the two plants in December of 1939 with Spencer Kellogg visible in the foreground.

In May of 1940 new storage space for the country's bountiful crops of soybeans was made available with the completion of 42 additional tanks at the Spencer-Kellogg Company's Decatur plant. The silos, built at a cost of about $100,000, were part of a long-range expansion program planned by the company in Decatur. The 115-foot high units tripled the plant storage space. More than two million bushels of soybeans were poured into the tanks at the start of the next harvest season. The site is at Brush College Road east of Decatur. ADM took over Spencer Kellogg in 1961.

Spencer Kellogg and Sons Philippines, Inc. The photo is dated December 8, 1939 the year that the minimum wage stood at 40 cents per hour; German forces were invading Poland and Czechoslovakia and nylon stockings first went on sale in America—before the outbreak of war.

ADM

The venerable Archer Daniels Midland was a direct successor to the turn-of-the-century Archer Daniels Linseed Company, formed by two old friends, George A. Archer and John W. Daniels, who grew up together in Ohio. By the time they opened up in Minneapolis, Archer, 55, and Daniels, 47, had had more than 50 years' experience between them in various linseed oil ventures. Frugal and formal, they saved incoming envelopes to use as scratch paper, and they addressed one another within a third party's hearing as "Mister."

In 1923, the firm became Archer Daniels Midland when the partners absorbed the Midland Linseed Products Company. ADM, with 344 presses in nine mills, became the largest linseed oil processor.

In 1939, Minneapolis-based Archer Daniels Midland Company acquired local buildings operated by Shellabarger, Spencer-Kellogg and Ralston Purina. The first soybeans were processed on September 25th of that year.

This unloading device, photo above, handled a freight car as though it were a toy as the first carload of soybeans arrived at the Archer Daniels Midland processing plant on September 26, 1939. The unloader tilts the car to one side and then forward and backward until all beans are poured out the door.

Closing a tank car at ADM on December 14, 1939, containing "gold from the soil." During this year's "rush" period, 8,000 - 9,000 carloads of soybeans were received.

A line of trucks waits to deliver soybeans to ADM on October 6, 1946. Soybeans were purchased from farmers throughout the Midwest. Currently ADM operates 165 plants in the Midwest that process soybeans, corn and wheat and other grains. The current chairman is Dwayne Andreas; Jim Randall serves as president.

ADM diversified into processing grain in 1927, and in 1929 it converted two linseed plants into soybean crushing. When the owners decided, in 1939, to build a plant specifically to handle soybeans, they selected Decatur as a site.

Shreve Archer was willing enough to commit himself and his firm's capital to faith in the potential of the soybean, despite his associates remembering, and respecting him as a cautious man.

After Shreve Archer's death, at only 47, in 1959, Thomas Daniels was in charge.

In 1933 Shreve M. Archer sent a representative to Europe to study the solvent extraction plants, and the next year started operating a 150-ton per day Hildebrandt continuous solvent extraction unit, thus becoming first in this country to produce soy products by that process.

While Archer Daniels Midland Company began processing by expeller in 1929, their big push in the industry came with entrance into the solvent extraction field, where they were first in volume production and merchandising of this type of 44 percent protein meal. In research work and merchandising of solvent-extracted soybean oil meal, long popular in Europe, they invested a great deal of capital.

Pictured is Richard Burket, longtime ADM spokesperson, at the Archer Daniels Midland hydroponics greenhouse on March 29, 1981.

Hydroponics is growing plants in water without using soil: nutrients are supplied in the water. Operating on a non-waste philosophy where all the energy is harnessed, ADM uses waste steam to operate 10 acres of greenhouses, then markets their produce, like lettuce and seedless cucumbers, to stores throughout the Midwest.

Over a period of years, ADM gradually moved management operations south until Decatur became the headquarters of the company in 1969. Company advertising proclaims the giant grain processor to be the "Supermarketer to the World."

Pictured is the original ADM soybean processing plant in Decatur (ADM East Plant). The new headquarters complex sits adjacent of the building in this photo that was shot on Valentine's Day in 1941.

Grain Processing

Frank M. Pratt, a prominent Decatur grain dealer, established the first transfer grain elevator in the town. Circa 1888 he and his brother entered the grain business in Decatur, opening branch offices in Chicago and Buffalo, New York In 1890 the brothers erected the Union Transfer Elevator, and later added a large mill in east Decatur for the manufacture of hominy and cereals.

The firm consolidated under the name of American Hominy Company in 1902. The brothers later formed the Pratt Cereal Oil Company which in turn became the Wellington Starch Works. Pratt moved to Texas in 1903, leaving his buildings empty.

Pratt Cereal processed the first cereal oil in the United States. The oil was used in the manufacture of soaps, paints, and salad oils; byproducts were corn starch and animal feed.

Pictured is the Pratt Cereal Mill, built in 1895 by the Pratt brothers, R.E. and Frank. A.E. Staley bought the land and buildings from American Hominy in 1919, and used it for storage until 1921 when it became the first of Staley's soybean processing plants. These buildings adjoined the starch plant purchased by Staley in 1909.

Decatur Cereal Mill, raised in 1907, produced the first breakfast food corn flakes which were sent to Battle Creek, Michigan for packaging. And from there to the grocery shelf. Suffern-Hunt was established by William H. Suffern (inset photo) and his cousin, Robert I. Hunt The pair were, from 1892-1898, grain traders in Decatur who took their considerable profits and opened their first mill at Union and the Wabash Railroad. The partners sold this mill in 1905 for $100,000 and raised the one pictured at West Eldorado and Van Dyck. It was the largest corn mill in the country with a maximum capacity of 15,000 bushels a day.

Office of the Decatur Cereal Company at West Eldorado and Van Dyke streets. The mill and the office were located on the site of what was later to become Polar Ice, currently Polar Water Products. After Suffern's mills burned down he went on to become the president of Polar Ice on the same site.

"Magnificent spectacle," quoted the newspaper. "There never has been a fire that could be seen in all its awful grandeur by so many people." Decatur's most spectacular fire was the burning of the Hunt-Suffern's Decatur Cereal Mill at the corner of Van Dyke and West Eldorado in 1909. Over $300,000 worth of damage was done to buildings, machinery and stock. Insurance covered only $160,000. The blaze was started in the top of the mill and burned itself out, out of reach of firemen who had a scant water supply, at best. The fire claimed the life of local firefighter, Jack Sheehy, father of four who was struck by falling timbers. The owners, Hunt and Suffern, watched the destruction of the mill with little emotion until the stricken firefighter was brought out.

Fire destroyed the Suffern-Hunt Mill of the American Hominy Company at North Union and the Wabash Railroad on November 27, 1913. The loss was estimated at $100,000 and was fully insured. Firefighters arrived at the blaze in two minutes. The fire started in the dryer room at the top of the mill. The two upper floors of the "Texas" elevator burned like tinder. One of the steel smokestacks became red hot. Garden hoses and buckets were used to drench and save nearby homes.

A 1939 aerial view of the A.E. Staley Manufacturing Plant in Decatur.

73

Staley's

Augustus Eugene Staley, Sr., founder and chief executive of A.E. Staley Manufacturing Company, was born on a farm near Julian, North Carolina in 1867. For 15 years, starting at age 17, he traveled as a salesman. He then settled in Baltimore and entered the starch business with $1500 in capital. His business expanded so rapidly that eastern competitors shut off his starch supply. At that point, he turned to the Corn Belt, looking for factory space to make his own starch.

In 1908 Staley heard about an inactive starch plant in Decatur, Illinois, and had the property appraised. He was told that coal was at the doorstep and all the corn he would need was within 75 miles of Decatur. Extensive repairs were made to the Wellington Starch Plant, and Staley's went on line at 7:00 a.m. on March 12, 1912. The soybean processing plant followed ten years later and was the first of its kind in America.

A. E. Staley

Pictured are 1901 Pratt Cereal Oil Company buildings which A.E. Staley purchased in 1909 from American Hominy (Indianapolis) and remodeled at a cost of $150,000 in 1912. The last of these buildings was recently razed.

The Staley plant is visible in the background showing Staley Field in the foreground. Located at the corner of Eldorado and 22nd streets, it was the center of the city's sports interest. It is currently a plant parking lot.

This older photo is possibly the starch table which ran the gluten starch milk along flumes to separate the heavier starch from the lighter gluten. Number 2 yellow dent corn was dumped into steep tanks, cleaned with water and sulfur dioxide.

Built in 1929 and 1930, the Staley headquarters was "an elaborate system of 200 floodlight projectors and copper reflectors with red, blue and amber lenses designed to furnish colored lighting and to illuminate the handsome edifice brilliantly at night."

"It was a contest in our family car when heading toward Decatur to see who would be the first to spot the Staley smokestacks. There was no prize given, but my parents had a few minutes of peace and quiet as we concentrated our eyes on the horizon in the direction of Decatur."

Only one stack remains standing today and is augmented by a co-generation plant.

Nighttime picture of the illuminated facade of the A.E. Staley office building. It is one of the most familiar landmarks to Decatur residents. Staley's dream was to erect an office building that would be a tribute to the loyalty and trust of his employees and customers.

Groundbreaking for the edifice took place on February 16, 1929. At 206 feet the facility was the tallest and most modern in downstate Illinois. It was often referred to as the "Lighthouse of the Prairie."

75

The walkway in 1950 to the Grain Processing Plant and to elevators C and D. In the processing plant soybeans were steamed, crushed and the hulls removed. The meat of the soybean was run through flaking rolls and into an extraction system to produce crude soybean oil and soybean meal.

Dust collectors (photo below) are an essential and valuable contribution to the milling industry for safety sake to protect the plant from explosion and the workers from dust inhalation.

Construction of storage elevator in September 1951. Workmen are shown atop the 231-foot-high workhouse at the A.E. Staley Manufacturing Company. The concrete structure was built with slip-forms similar to those used on new grain bins shown in the background. Work progressed at an average of approximately 16 feet a day. The headhouse (the concrete rooftop structure) that houses the conveyor moves the grain from one silo to another or from the silo to production.

The A.E. Staley Manufacturing Company was bought out in 1988 by Tate & Lyle, PLC, of London, England.

Representative Products of the A.E. Staley Manufacturing Co.

Courtesy of *Herald & Review*

A LIST OF STALEY PRODUCTS IN 1928:

Pure Food Starches
Mill Starches
Thin Boilng Starch
Cream Corn Starch
Laundry Starch
Soy Bean Meal
Soy Bean Health Flour
Soy Bean Oil
Stayco Gum
Poster Paste
Corn Syrups (Unmixed)
Corn Sugars
Table Syrups
Corn Gluten Feed
Perfect Protein Feed
Corn Germ Meal
Corn Oil
Salad and Cooking Oil
Soft Soaps

Shellabarger

Incorporated in 1888 with capital stock of $250,000, Shellabarger Mill & Elevator was established by D.S. Shellabarger who had been involved in Decatur milling since 1856, first with Hinkle, Shellabarger & Company, then with the Great Western Mill. As sole proprietor D.S. Shellabarger gave to his three sons, W.L., F.D., and L.C., an equal share in the business.

David S. Shellabarger, born in 1837 and died in 1913, set in motion the Shellabarger industrial empire. He married Anna E. Krone, daughter of pioneer druggist, Nathan Krone, in 1862. David organized Shellabarger Milling in 1856 and the Shellabarger Elevator in 1903. He served as president of the National Bank of Decatur.

William Lincoln Shellabarger was secretary and manager for the Decatur division of the midwestern conglomerate, American Hominy, dry corn millers, formerly managed locally by his father, D.S. In 1904 he took over Shellabarger Elevator Company, establishing a line of mills and elevators in central Illinois.

On October 23, 1929, the first day of the stock market crash, Shellabarger Grain Products began soybean processing. When built, the tanks designed for soybean storage, had a total capacity of 80,00 bushels. The plant was located along the spur track from the Illinois Central Railroad line, north of the Wabash Railroad on Brush College Road. Photo from June 6, 1940. In the early '50s Shellabarger sold out to Ralston Purina who eventually sold to ADM.

In 1888 the business had an old fashioned stone mill with two pairs of burrs, one for wheat and the other for corn. The mill's daily output was 125 barrels.

Shellabarger Mill and Pratt Cereal combined to form an American Hominy Company in May, 1902 and capitalized at $3.5 million. Daily capacity of the graining enterprise was 85,000 bushels of corn.

By 1934 Shellabarger, like other Illinois farmers, had gotten on the soybean track. Thanks to a destructive sweep of chinch bugs which killed grain fields farmers began investing heavily in soybeans.

The soybean was taking its rightful place as a major crop second only to corn.

Fire destroyed a soybean experimental building at the Shellabarger plant in June 1934.

Workers filling 100-pound bags of soybean flour at Shellabarger Grain Products in 1934.

How the Shellabargers Came

Two young men by the name of Shellabarger came to Illinois on horseback in 1836. They were cousins and their names were Isaac and John. They were around twenty years of age. They had been born in Pennsylvania and they left their folks there and set out toward the west because they had heard of the success that was possible to youth and enterprise in the new state of Illinois. Their good star guided them to the county of Macon, and they entered 160 acres of land, mostly timber.

David Shellabarger was a brother of Isaac. He was also a miller, like his father, whose name was originally Von Schellenburg. He was a Swiss. To this David Shellabarger, miller, and his wife, was born a son, July 11, 1837, and he was named David.

Young David Shellabarger worked around his father's mill until he was nineteen years old. Then he decided to follow his uncle Isaac to Illinois. He arrived in Decatur the evening of May 28, 1856, on the first Wabash train from Tolono. When he came to town he worked in a lumber yard and was satisfied with the $1.25 which he received as pay. But it wasn't long before his thrift made it possible for him to buy an interest in the business which he disposed of in 1859. [E.B. Hitchcock]

Some Decatur businesses that have existed 50 years or more:

A. E. Staley Manufacturing
Aratex Means Services
Archer Daniels Midland
Architectural Iron Works of Decatur
Bachrachs
Barnett Sign Service
Benson Creamery
Black and Company
Blue Mill Restaurant
Bodine Electric
Burks Pumps
Christy-Foltz Inc.
Citizens National Bank
   (now First Bank of America)
Day's Paint Store
Decatur and Macon County Hospital
   (now Decatur Memorial)
Decatur Sanitary District
Del's Popcorn Shop
First National Bank of Decatur
Fisher-Stoune Inc.
Folrath Shoe Store
Frazier Signs
Grigoleit Grohne Concrete Products
Heinkel's Packing
Herald & Review Newspaper
Hooker Glass and Paint
Huston-Patterson Corp.
Illinois Bell Telephone
Illinois Power
K's Merchandise Mart
Millikin Bank
J.J. Moran Funeral Home
Mueller Company
National System of Garage Ventilation
Ornamental Metalworks
Owen Press Printers/Mr. Rush Printing
Prairie Farms Dairy
Purity Baking
St. Mary's Hospital
J. J. Swartz Company
Thompson Decatur Lumber
Tom's Grill
Traver Supply Inc.
Union Iron Works
Wagner Castings
Wallender Wedman Printing
WSOY

Contrary to popular legend the pioneers were not totally self-sufficient. They needed cast iron kettles, skillets, guns, augers, nails and ax heads not to mention household goods and essentials like coffee, salt, dyes, ready-made cloth and the all-purpose cure-all—medicinal whiskey. William Cantrell, who opened the first general store, soon had competition as specialty stores (green grocers, dry goods) pushed out general stores offering a wider selection of merchandise. Competition from chain stores challenged by 1910: the five and tens as well as Montgomery Ward and J.C. Penney. Before the Civil War the market was the agricultural community. Merchants ordered their goods with an eye on crop condition. After the Civil War retailers targeted a market of city shoppers. Neighborhood retail centers sprung up providing drug, barber and restaurant services. After World War II chain stores bought in bulk pushing out locally owned stores. The space needs of the superstores and parking needs of shoppers drew merchandisers to outlying area. First came the strip mall then indoor malls anchored by large stores. Retailing had come full circle so that many stores became like the original general stores carrying a little bit of everything.

William Cantrell Comes
Early in 1833 William Cantrell moved from Springfield to Decatur, bringing with him the first general merchandise stock that ever came to Decatur. Uncle Jimmy Renshaw's stock, judging from the items charged in his account book was as general as anyone could wish, but his place was more like a frontier trading post, a place of barter. William Cantrell established a real store. [E.T. Coleman]

Few Cash Transactions
There were not many cash transactions and in lieu of cash many things were acquired in trade. There were pork, pelts, cowhides, vegetables, eggs, wild game, and deer, turkey, ducks and geese were brought in and duly credited to the man who brought them. The credit was liberal and the prices were fair. [E.T. Coleman]

First Entry
That old account book of Uncle Jimmy Renshaw's is still in existence and it is a veritable mine of information. The first entry in this book was a credit to William Hanks for 104 pounds of fresh-killed pork, for which he was allowed a cent and a half a pound to be taken out in trade.
Other settlers brought in things in trade. Lewis Ward thus disposed of fifty-five pounds of deer skins at eighteen cents a pound; Samuel McKay came in with seventeen pounds of beef hide, for which he received a total credit of $1.32. William King brought two bushels of mortar-broken, for which he was credited all of fifty cents. [E.T. Coleman]

Downton Decatur rooftops in the 1930s. The Linn & Scruggs building is prominent, as is the back of the Lincoln Theater advertising both Vaudeville and motion pictures. And to the left, the top of the Transfer House is just visible.

In July 1930, this was how Decatur looked on North Water Street. This view is looking north up the street. Many old Decatur businesses include the Prince, Bijou and Empress theaters. Note that *The Arizona Kid* is playing at the Empress.

Decatur Circa 1890

Top Left: J.G. Starr & Son Harness Company

Top Right: Shellabarger Mill and Elevator Company

Bottom Left: Heuver and Giddons Shoe Manufactury

Bottom Right: D.R. Alexander and Company

Top Left: Decatur Coal Shaft Company

Top Middle: Decatur Union Elevator

Top Right: Decatur Ice Factory and Cold Storage Company

Bottom Left: Decatur Brewing Company

Bottom Right: Lyon and Armstrong Company Planing Mills

Top left: Union Iron
Works

Top right: The
Wayne Sulkyette &
Road Cart
Company

Bottom left:
Gallagher Block

Bottom right:
Woman's Club
Building

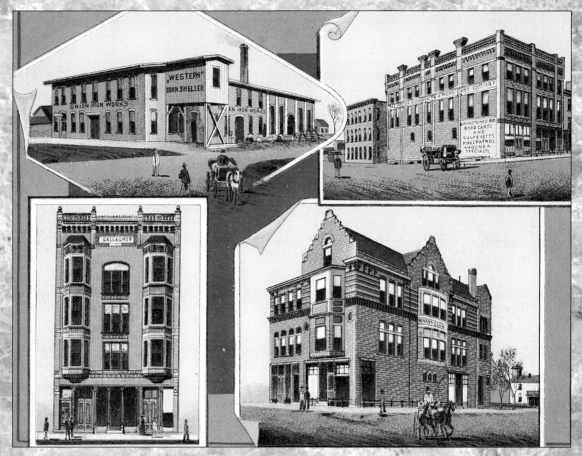

Top Left: H. Mueller
& Sons

Top Middle: In the
Library Block is
Sorgen &
Stewart
Cornice Works
and Smith &
Hubbards
Laboratory

Top Right:
    H. Mueller &
    Sons Plumbers

Bottom Left:
    Millikin Bank

Bottom Middle:
    Haworth Block

Bottom Right:
    H. Mueller
    Manufacturing
    Company

Early Businessmen

Hugh W. Hill came to Macon County in 1866. Hill was a farmer, and brought no capital with him when he made the move to the county. He leased a farm nine miles outside of Decatur. A problem occurred with Hill's hogs that led to his invention of an item that gave him business success. The hogs would root in Hill's cultivated pasture land. He experimented with a method to ring their noses to prevent them from rooting up the ground. The result was the hog ringer. Hill did not have the means to manufacture and market his product, so he formed a partnership with Charles P. Housum. H. W. Hill and Company then began a massive advertising campaign of the product. Customers came from all over the world, and Hill realized financial success beyond dream and expectation. Hill eventually sold his interest in the company,

Orville B. Gorin was the son of financier, Jerome R. Gorin. Born on January 25, 1849, Orville attended Knox College in Galesburg, Illinois. He returned to Decatur and accepted a position in the James Millikin and Company Bank in 1865. Gorin became a partner in 1880, buying out his father's interest in the bank. In October 1897 the bank was incorporated as the Millikin National Bank, with James Millikin as president, O. B. Gorin as its cashier, while his father, Jerome R., served as sole proprietor along with James Millikin and J. M. Brownback as assistant cashier. At James Millikin's death in 1909, Orville became bank president .

Jerome R. Gorin, born October 12, 1817, was a law partner of three famous local judges, a banker for 30 years and a state representative. Gorin arrived in Decatur in 1833 at age 16, a year after the Black Hawk War. Decatur was a tiny village on the western frontier. He helped found two of Decatur's prominent banking institutions: Millikin Bank and Citizens National Bank (now First of America). Mr. Gorin began his career at 16 working as a salesman. In 1842 he studied law for two years. After admission to the bar, Gorin prepared legal work for the city and also worked in partnership with Judge Arthur

Gallagher until 1861. Millikin and Oder established their banking firm in that year, and Gorin served as cashier. In 1865 he became a partner with James Millikin but continued in his capacity as cashier until 1881, establishing his own firm of Gorin and Bills. The private banking institution handled loans as well as real estate. The partnership ended in 1883 when Gorin opened the banking firm of Gorin and Dawson. He sold out to L. B. Casner, and the institution merged with Citizens National Bank. A year later Gorin became the bank president. He retired in 1892, and sold his interest in the bank.

John W. Culver was a native of Christian County, Illinois, and moved to Decatur in 1889. In 1891, Culver opened a small electrical supply house. Shortly after this, R. F. Piatt obtained a franchise from the city to provide commercial lighting. Culver and his business associates had signed the note for Piatt's business. It failed, and Culver and his partners fell heir to the franchise. Culver along with a J. M. Willard formed the Municipal Electric Company. Acquiring a site at Cerro Gordo and Edward streets, the partners raised the first plant in Decatur to provide alternating electric current. Culver also introduced meters to measure electricity consumption. The meter

rate was 15 cents per kilowatt hour. Residents paid an average of $2.50 a month for electricity in the 1890s.

Poor health convinced Culver to seek a change of climate in Florida in 1895. When he returned to Decatur several months later, the Municipal Electric Company was in receivership. One of Culver's brothers bought Willard's interest, and the brothers formed Culver Electric in 1897. The company consolidated with George Danforth's Decatur Electric Company and the Decatur Gas and Light to form Decatur Gas and Electric Company in 1898. Danforth bought the brothers out a year later.

Nathan L. Krone was a notable Decatur pioneer for many reasons: but besides being a druggist in Decatur for over 60 years; perhaps he is best known for first bringing "white oil" (kerosene) to the town circa 1860 to make heating and lighting easier for local residents. At the time, the townspeople were experimenting with various other oil mixtures, but they were meeting no success because these other fuels like Camphene (a fuel distilled from turpentine) were explosive. When Krone brought his first barrel of the "white oil" to Decatur, it was out of reach financially for many at a cost of $2.25 a gallon. However, a short time later, Krone purchased 50 barrels, enough to last the city six months and to allow him to drop the price to $1.00 per gallon.

Krone came to Decatur in 1839 from central Pennsylvania when he was seven years old. He and his parents had the experience of navigating an incredibly difficult water route to finally arrive in the then wild frontier of Illinois.

Nathan Krone's childhood home was the Macon House

(later the Revere House). There he had the opportunity to meet many important visitors to the town. He lived his entire life in Decatur during some of the most exciting times in the city's history. He saw the pre-railroad period, the building of the first two railroads and the arrival of the first train in Decatur. He also saw the Mexican, Civil and Spanish-American wars and the first years of World War I.

Nathan Krone knew Abraham Lincoln and was at the state convention on South Park Street where Lincoln was first named for the presidency. He was also involved in the business affairs of the city. In regard to his personal career, he ran the Macon House, was employed by local stores, and eventually went into business for himself. He erected two downtown buildings where he and his son plied their druggist trade until 1915.

Nathan Krone's daughter, Anna, eventually married David S. Shellabarger, the head of one of the most extensive milling concerns in the midwest.

Pictured is the east side of Lincoln Square, at the Merchant and Main Street intersection. O and W Company is having a bankrupt sale. One-Price Clothing House advertises on the corner store indicating the price of a dress is no longer negotiable. Also visible are Lewis Moore, a physician's office, a saloon and the horseshoe on the corner facility wishing "Good Luck to all who enter here."

A view on Water Street. The corner structure housed a dental parlor and King's Drug Store.

Brenneman building at 148-154 North Franklin was owned by D. W. Brenneman, a wholesale liquor company. Space was also let to Decatur Auction and Furniture Company. To the right is a pool hall and saloon.

The Library Block, 100 block of East William. Note the streetcar tracks. "Trolley parties were the rage. Gay young folks chartered a car for an evening, and had a big thrill in going over the street car lines."

The Syndicate and Pasfield buildings at 234 to 250 North Main Street. The taller Syndicate building on the left is home to Norman's Laundry and Barbers (believed to be the first steam laundry in the state.) Norman's was also a 10-chair barber shop with 18 bathing rooms which took in commercial and residential laundry. The Pasfield professional building appears on the right. The top floor of the Pasfield housed an architect, I. O. Stein. Other offices included Drs. Walsh, C. B. Smith and Meyers plus Stafford & Patterson Real Estate, Loans and Insurance.

It appears that a sale at Gushart's Dry Goods and Millinery was drawing a crowd at the corner of East Prairie and North Water Street in 1896.

Checkrowers

The leading industry of Decatur was the manufacture of checkrowers, an attachment to the power corn planter, which checks the cross rows at regular intervals so that the corn may be cultivated two ways. Previous to that the corn planter was a two-man implement, one man driving the team and the other operating the dropper. In addition to that the field had to be marked for the cross rows before the actual planting could begin, and the marking was as big a job as the planting.

The invention of the checkrower gave enormous impetus to the growing of corn. The vital feature of the invention was at first a knotted rope and later a knotted wire.

This invention was the beginning of much industrial development in Decatur. With it began the making of various agricultural implements. For a time the manufacture of these implements was the leading industry in Decatur. It all began with the making of a corn planter in Decatur by G.D. Haworth and invention of the checkrower by him. [E.T. Coleman]

Early Hotels in Decatur

"The leading hotel back in 1839 was the Macon House which was later included in the Revere House. There was also the Oglesby House, the Cloudas and the St. Nicholas. We know that Will Oglesby came here in 1855 by steamer up the Mississippi to St. Louis then overland to Decatur. His wife was Zerelda Glore and they were married in Kentucky. There were three older children besides the present Mrs. Montgomery: Dick Oglesby, who later became an actor and was mysteriously killed in Missouri; Annie, who married George Downing; and little Blanche, who was killed by falling through the banisters at the Oglesby House.

When his child was killed in his hotel, Willis Oglesby gave up the business which had not proved very profitable to him anyway. He enlisted and was killed on the second day of the Battle of Shiloh. His widow lived on Cerro Gordo Street, in the last house on the street, between Church and Union, and Mrs. Montgomery remembers that her mother always had a light in the window and wakened her little group of children when soldier trains went by."

From an early newspaper account.

Revere dinner tables "groaned with food." A sample dinner in 1866 included oyster soup, salmon with lobster sauce, leg of mutton with egg sauce, pig stuffed with bread crumbs, stewed tomatoes, lobster salad and plum pudding with rum sauce. Dieting was not fashionable.

The Revere House. Lincoln stayed here when riding the circuit and "helped Mrs. Johns, a long term hotel resident, move her piano in." First called the Macon House, the facility was built on the southeast corner of Prairie and Franklin streets by Captain David L. Allen and Dr. Thomas H. Read. For 30 years it was the leading hotel and the center of social activity in Decatur, and a draw for east side business. When the hotel burned in 1871, business in the New Square area declined.

Fistfights at the Revere Hotel

In the days of the old Decatur Rolling mill there was a healer who was a good man and was fully aware of it. He was an experienced scrapper and he would have given a trained prize fighter a run for his money.

In Decatur there was a blacksmith who was a pretty husky guy himself and he did not care who knew it. He is still living here and therefore is not named. One Sunday afternoon the two met in front of the old Revere house at Franklin and Prairie streets. There was no quarrel and grudge to satisfy. The probability is that they had never met before. As soon as the matter of identity had been settled satisfactorily, they stripped their coats and blithely went to it.

They were both in the heavyweight class, lithe and muscular, and hard and experienced fighters. They were in as good condition as Gene Tunney when he steps into the ring. The inevitable human ring quickly formed and the mighty battle was on. Not a policeman or sheriff's officer interfered.

Both the combatants could stand a tremendous amount of punishment. Blows in plenty landed and they were not love taps, but neither seemed to have what is known in modern ring parlance as the knockout punch. They fought till both were bloody as stuck pigs. They were so evenly matched that neither gained an advantage, but they fought on and on till neither could fight any more. They were both completely exhausted. The battle was a draw but it was a battle that went down in history. [E.T. Coleman]

For more than half a century hotels were numerous in the area near the railroad depots. The National Hotel (photo 1889) was the first of these raised on Front Street. A two-story brick at the southwest corner of Cerro Gordo and Front streets, the hostelry, was operated by John McEvoy. In 1907 the facility was replaced by the Kraft Hotel. At the left was a newsstand operated by Louis Chadot, Sr., where he also sold soft drinks and tobacco.

"Landy" or Landa Harrell kept the Smock Boarding House at 432 East Main Street, erected in 1882 by Henry Smock. His wife "Landlady" Harrell had earlier run the Revere House, first known as the "Social Hall." The structure was condemned by the city council in 1934 to be torn down or moved away. Photo circa 1930.

St. Nicholas Hotel

The St. Nicholas was recognized as one of the leading hotels in central Illinois in 1887. Established in 1865 by Charles Laux, the hotel contained 70 sleeping rooms, "well ventilated, lighted and equipped for the comfort of guests." Located in the central part of the city, the hotel had all the modern conveniences of its day. It was said that the hotel had one of the finest billiard rooms outside the city of Chicago. An early sign on top of the St. Nick proclaimed it to be fireproof. It has indeed survived the years, undergone renovation and currently serves as home to a restaurant and business offices.

The original site was built by Dr. Speer as a hotel called the "Social Hall" and was run by the "worthy" landlady Harrell. It was the spillover place when the Revere House was full but nevertheless served as a hospitable, bountiful hotel. Even a fiddler provided tunes for a "ball" and the patrons danced; "the men wore boots with pants inside the tops." Raising the "hall," precursor to the St. Nicholas bankrupted the builder, Dr. Speer.

The three-story hotel before it came into the possession of Nicholas, Peter and Charles Laux was also known as the Harrell, Oglesby and the Cloudas House. (Willis Oglesby was uncle to Governor Richard Oglesby.) The Lauxs were innovators introducing three kerosene lamps to light stairways. To guide coaches driving from the railroad station a lantern was hung in a top floor window. The hotel remained in the Laux family until 1953 making it the oldest organization in America run by one family. The Ayde Corp took over and remodeled the newer part of the hotel in 1964.

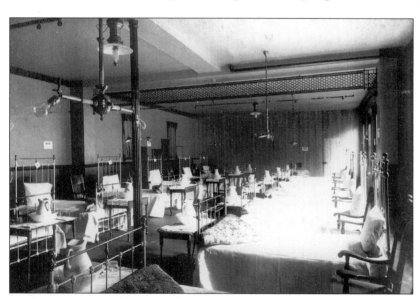

In 1904 the old St. Nicholas converted its billiard room into a dormitory. Besides private rooms, non-private less expensive dormitory style rooms were also offered.

Inset: Charles A. Laux founded the St. Nicholas Hotel in 1865 with his brother, Nicholas. He retired from the hotel business in 1911 and turned it over to his sons, James and Clark. That same year he was elected vice-president of the Illinois State Hotel Association.

Left: A 1953 exterior shot of the St. Nicholas Hotel, a landmark that was located on Main Street. Part of the St. Nicholas Hotel was torn down in 1966 to make room for the Ambassador Motor Inn on South Main Street.

Two chefs ply their culinary trade in the St. Nicholas Hotel kitchen on November 29, 1934. The St. Nicholas was the place to go for a nice dinner on a special day.

Luggage in the St. Nicholas Hotel baggage room in the early 1900s.

A nostalgic view of the square with the St. Nicholas Hotel shown to the right of and behind the Transfer House (south and west) on May 11, 1953.

In this stately hotel the Grand Army of the Republic of Civil War veterans framed their original constitution in 1866. When Charles Laux (the brother who ended up running the hotel) died in 1914, he was recognized as the dean of hotel men in the country having run the St. Nicholas or "Saint Nicholaux" for 52 years.

A postcard view of the lobby of the Hotel Orlando. The hotel was converted into senior citizens' apartments in 1982.

The Hotel Orlando, circa 1928, had 250 rooms, 200 of them with baths. Rates started at $2.00 a day. The hostelry had three air-conditioned restaurant rooms: the Commodore, English Coffee and the Venetian. Decatur's largest hotel, the Orlando was built in 1915 at a cost of $375,000 on the site of the Powers Opera House that had burned twice on the northeast corner of Water and Wood streets. The Powers family has played a prominent role in the development of Decatur and the state of Illinois since 1839. Through land holdings and varied business endeavors including his investment in the resplendent Decatur Opera House, Orlando Powers became one of the wealthiest men Macon County had produced. Orlando's grandson, Jack H., one of Decatur's top civic and professional leaders, took over the hotel in 1946 before leasing it to Boss Hotels in 1956. A major addition and extensive remodeling programs have been completed over the years.

The Angle Hotel at 519 North Front Street was one of the early hotels and the third on Front Street in the center of activity near the old Wabash Railroad and the Illinois Central. Built in the early 1900s, it was renovated in 1911 and finally torn down in 1958.

The second of the Front Street hotels was the Kraft, located at Cerro Gordo, replacing the National Hotel in 1907. Many may remember that Dante's Italian Village, a popular restaurant and nighttime entertainment spot, later located in this former hostelry. On November 16, 1987 a fire broke out at 2:30 a.m. in this uninsured building. It required five fire engines to bring the blaze under control.

George W. Kraft established the Kraft Hotel in 1907. A true entrepreneur, he also owned the Whistle Bottling Works, served as captain of the volunteer fire department and was part owner of three gold mines in Colorado.

Telephone Service

Lowber Burrows, Decatur's first real banker, came home from Yale with Decatur's first telephone in 1879—three years after Alexander Graham Bell had exhibited his invention in Philadelphia. He set up a line between his home and that of J. E. Bering who lived a half block away.

The first real telephone line was put up by James W. Haworth, the farm implement manufacturer, to connect his office with his factory.

In October 1879, Western Union established a telephone exchange. The city population was 10,000 and there were 33 local telephone customers. By 1883 Decatur had three competing telephone companies; Bell, American Bell and Central Union, providing service to 151 customers. By 1912, there were two companies left, Decatur Home and Central Union. The fierce competition for customers continued until Central Union purchased Decatur Home in 1917; the company then had 8,000 subscribers. Illinois Bell came into existence in 1920 when Central Union and Chicago Bell merged. On December 1, 1920, Illinois Bell came to Decatur to serve the city's 10,204 customers. The company was located at 132 East North Street from 1903-1929 and moved to 201 East North Street in 1929.

Decatur Home Telephone succeeded the Macon County Telephone and the earlier Citizens Mutual Telephone in 1907, and raised this imposing edifice at 223 North Main Street in 1908. Nine years later, it was absorbed by Central Union, the Illinois Bell predecessor.

The Decatur Home Telephone building in February 1950. After a century of telephone use, the city of Decatur had, by 1979, advanced from a single telephone in use to almost 100,000 according to Illinois Bell Telephone.

The Central Union Telephone Company toll board in 1904. This board was located on the second floor at 132 East North Street. During this era, money for service rendered was brought in by collectors. It was not until 1914 that bills were distributed by mail.

Illinois Bell Telephone Company operators in May 1961. At this time there was no charge for information calls.

Empty boards at Illinois Bell. The operators went on strike four months after Victory in Japan Day in November of 1945. Management was dispatched to "fill in."

Lighting Decatur

The Barnum and Bailey Circus gave Decatur its first look at electricity—brilliant arc lights—in 1880. Silas T. Trowbridge organized an electric company in 1883, Decatur Electric Light Company. City streets were lighted first by arc lamps, erected on towers. By 1886, eight of the towers lighted the city at night. The late 19th century saw four power companies come and go. By 1900 the Decatur Gas and Electric Company, run by George Danforth, emerged as the front-runner in providing electricity to city residents. Gas lighting was replaced with electric lights, and the eight towers became obsolete. Corner streetlights were installed and commercial lighting went into stores and saloons.

Industry began to demand electrical service, and the growth was too fast for the privately owned Decatur Gas and Electric Company. In 1903, the com-

pany united with the Decatur Street Railway Company to become the Decatur Light and Railway Company. The invention of new appliances as well as industries requiring electricity resulted in a supply that could not keep up with the demand. In 1923 the Decatur Railway and Light Company consolidated with other power companies in order to generate electrical power from a centralized source. The larger company was known as the Illinois Power and Light Company later to become Illinois Power. Illinois Power and Light had holdings in Iowa as well as Illinois, but in 1945 divested itself of the out-of-state properties to operate solely in Illinois. In 1939, the headquarters were moved from Champaign-Urbana to Decatur.

Men waiting to help customers at the information window inside the Decatur Railway and Light Company.

Offices of the Decatur Railway and Light Company in December 1910.

An illuminated Transfer House in December 1910, lit courtesy of the Decatur Railway and Light Company. The 125-foot arc light electric tower that had provided the city's first nighttime lighting in 1886 had been moved in 1906 to make room for the Transfer House in Lincoln Square. Farmers were relieved. They complained that driving towards Decatur, the lights blinded them. Mothers worried that when their sons climbed the towers they wouldn't be able to get down.

The Decatur Railway and Light Company power plant in 1909, located at the northwest corner of North Edward and Cerro Gordo streets. This photo was taken before the new smokestack was built. Quite a change from the 50-horsepower engine that served as Decatur's first power plant in 1883 on Wabash Avenue.

Illinois-Iowa Power Company building at 134 East Main Street on December 19, 1948.

Illinois Power and Light Company sub-station in June of 1940. Foundations were being constructed for an addition as part of the utility's expansion program which included a 138,000 volt line into the substation.

99

Cigars

Cigar-making was one of the top industries in Decatur at the turn of the century. There were 22 factories in the city including Michl's Tobacco Company, Decatur Cigar, Osborn Brothers Cigar, Lincoln Square Cigar and Palmeyer Cigar. Many tobacconists were of German descent. Joseph Michl and Henry Shlaudeman opened Michl's in January 1858. The company remained in business for over a hundred years and occupied one of the oldest buildings in Decatur at 120 North Water Street. The business was sold in 1974 but continued operations under the same name. Progress took its toll. The business closed in 1980 and was torn down to make way for a new plaza area for First National Bank of Decatur.

This photograph of Michl's Cigar Manufacturing Company ran in the *Review* on September 13, 1908. In 1900, 22 cigar factories employed 135 producing five million cigars annually as well as snuff, chewing and pipe tobacco.

Michl's Cigar Store interior in 1912. It even looks aromatic. The strategically located cuspidors "encouraged" customers not to spit on the floor.

Man showing molds at Michl's in December 1958, the centennial year of Joseph Michl & Sons. Michl had originally established his wholesale and retail dealership employing seven men. After World War I the popularity of cigarettes plus the advent of cigar-making machines curtailed the industry, and a few businesses like Michl's survived.

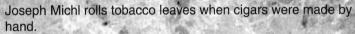

Joseph Michl rolls tobacco leaves when cigars were made by hand.

Many cigar operations were a one-man plant with the proprietor doing all the work. An exception was the John Keck Company in 1881 on the corner of West Wood and South Church which employed 17 on its saws, planes and presses. Paper boxes for local trade and cigar boxes for manufacturers were also produced.

Incorrectly believed to reside in front of Michl's Cigar Store when in reality the noble Indian, pictured in March 1953, guarded the northwest corner of Main and Prairie.

The 100 block of West Prairie, showing the corner where the cigar store Indian once stood.

Muhlenbruch Glove Company located at 331 North Main Street. Otto Muhlenbruch moved his glove and mitten factory from Ven Wert, Ohio, in 1906 with the express purpose of having access to a larger market of female workers to produce leather and cloth goods. Male workers were used previously. On December 14, 1922, Otto's son, C.H., declared the firm bankrupt but tried to resume work despite insolvency. Muhlenbruch's operated in Decatur for 17 years.

I am almost done my cotten. We have some planted but the summer is so short I am afraid we will not make much. If we do we will have to make a gin of our fingers or take it 50 miles to a better one. We have to put up with many inconveniences we would not have had in an oalder settlement; we have no doctor, no preacher, no water grist mill, no saw mill, no cotten gin nor tan yard, but I hope we will lack none of these things long. [We came to Decatur] in March [1829]. We give ten dollars for one cow, she is large and fat. She has a heiffer calf and gives us plenty of milk. This has been a verry dry spring. We have seen little rain since we left Tennessee. The sope we brought with us lasted till we made more.
[Marilla Martin Baker, early pioneer]

Women folding linens at Model Laundry at 302 North Franklin Street.

Women entered the workforce in jobs they normally were responsible for at home: making and cleaning clothes, millinery, hotels and hospitality. Garment and woolen textile manufacturing have long occupied a prominent place in Decatur industrial history. Home Manufacturing Company started making cotton dresses in Decatur in 1895. Pictured here are garment factory workers.

Women at Work

Work of Women - Pioneer Style

The women of the household carded and spun their own flax and wool, wove it into fabric and fashioned the fabric into clothing. Spinning wheels and reels and winding blades, and looms were common household necessities, the last named occupying more space than a grand piano. Yet these women managed to find time to do all the work and more. House-keeping? There were no mysteries about it where an entire large family were crowded into one or two rooms.

These pioneers ground their own corn in improvised mortars. They roofed their houses with three-foot shingles derived from fine, straight grained whiteoak splints and baskets were made of the same material. By slightly varying the process of making the splints brooms were sometimes made in a pinch. Bedsteads were quickly made in an emergency of a few poles with an ax and an auger.

The women made their own soap with lye leached from wood ashes, and their own starch from wheat bran. Yet these women did not seem to know that they were enduring hardships. [E.B. Hitchcock]

Interior of a beauty parlor. The permanent rods hanging at rear right were used to "bob" hair during the "Roaring '20s. Women were called into men's work domain during World War II. (Photos this page from Decatur Public Library Charles Wasson Collection)

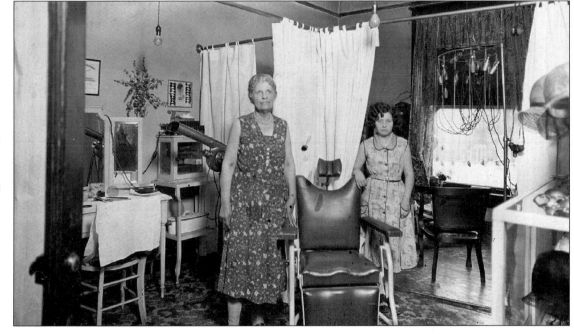

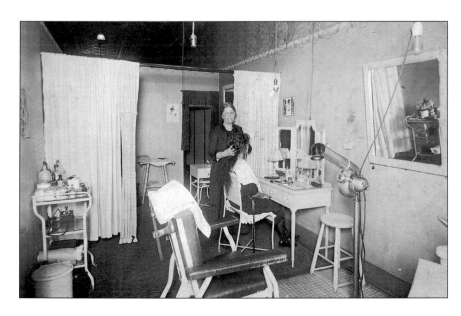

Another beauty parlor view. It appears it might be a makeshift parlor in a home. Notice the vanity table the woman is sitting at, and the hanging light bulbs. The common belief was that electricity was safer if the wires were visible.

103

Banking in Decatur

Decatur banking had its start in a general store opened in 1836 by J. J. Peddecord in the 100 block of East Main Street. Evidently Peddecord had proved himself trustworthy as his fellow townsmen handed over surplus cash to him in his store for safekeeping. By 1856 Peddecord and his partner, Lowber Burrows, sold the store and went into banking full time becoming the first exclusive banking institution in Decatur and Macon County.

The "Big Three," Citizens, Millikin and First National, dominated the city's banking scene for well over a hundred years. However, in October of 1955, a permit was issued to charter a fourth bank, the Soy Capital Bank and Trust.

Soy Capital was the brainchild of Walter Morey, a Decatur native and Harvard law graduate who returned to Decatur to work for A. E. Staley Manufacturing. In 1955 he selected the south side of the 1500 block of East Eldorado Street, a site the bank maintains today. Morey currently serves as chairman

of the board; Robert C. Smith, president; Larry Jackson, senior vice-president; Larry E. Ramey, senior vice-president; Gary C. House, senior vice-president; and Ki Kim, vice-president and senior trust officer.

Morey organized Security Savings and Loan Association in 1960 which sold in 1983 to Gem City Savings and Loan from Quincy, Illinois. In 1990 Gem City fell victim to federal regulations. Soy Capital took over all deposits of the two Decatur branches of Gem City. Morey again found himself serving as chairman of his former institution.

Savings and loan institutions had entered the Decatur banking scene as early as 1881 with the People's Savings and Loan Association occupying quarters downtown. Mutual Home and Savings was also one of the first savings and loan establishments in the city and opened for business in 1904. The institution has been at the same location at 135 East Main Street since 1926. The name changed to First Mutual Savings

Bank in 1989. Current president and chief executive officer is Paul K. Reynolds; Dave Weber, senior vice-president; Phil Duffy, senior vice-president; G. Lynn Brinkman, vice-president and chief financial officer; Gary M. Walters, vice-president; Jim W. Goatley, vice-president; and John Weakley, vice-president.

Credit Unions are a product of the 20th century. The Decatur Wabash Employees Credit Union was the first to organize in 1927. Other employers in the city have organized credit unions over the years: Caterpillar Inc., A. E. Staley's, Mueller Company, Firestone and others. Some have lost their singular identity through mergers with larger entities. Caterpillar's credit union is now Decatur Earthmover Credit Union. Mueller's is currently known as First Community Credit Union. Early credit unions were established to benefit employees only but the concept has now broadened to encompass the entire community.

This photo depicts the Citizens National Bank employees at the bank's remodeling celebration on June 11, 1948. The bank extended open house observances over a five-day period to local bankers, schoolchildren, customers and friends. The renovation of the former facility, begun in 1946, resulted in twice the floor space. More than 2,000 children lined up around the building to take a tour of the bank and receive free movie tickets to see either *Geronimo* or *The Adventures of Huckleberry Finn*.

First National Bank

The Decatur National Bank opened in 1873 with Robert Hervey as president and with capital stock of $100,000. In 1893 the name changed to National Bank of Decatur. National Bank bought out Lowber Burrows and Company in 1912, erecting its current building on the site of the former Burrow's bank at Park and Water streets. After that acquisition Decatur's oldest financial institution became the first Decatur bank to be nationally chartered.

Decatur National changed its name to First

Decatur National Bank's original location at the northwest corner of Prairie and Water streets from 1890-1900.

Below: Decatur National Bank erected an impressive edifice at South Park and Water streets in 1914. Stately ionic columns were a defining feature of this classic-style structure.

National Bank in 1966. In 1979 a holding company was formed, First Decatur Bancshares, Inc., with First National as its only subsidiary.

Early success of the bank was tied to the growth of the railroads throughout the Midwest in the 19th century. This century has seen the bank prosper through the community's involvement in agriculture and industry.

Tom R. Dickes currently serves as chairman of the board with John W. Luttrell as chief executive officer and president; Milton Brahier, senior vice-president of lending; Pete Grosso, senior vice-president of personal banking and cashier; and Matt Graves, vice-president and financial officer.

Main lobby of First National Bank as it appeared before renovation in 1976.

A walk-up window for customer convenience in 1954 proved easier than standing in line inside the bank on a busy lunch hour.

The elegant lobby of Decatur National Bank at the South Park and Water streets location when the interior was completed circa 1914.

Magna Bank

Decatur's second bank was opened in 1860 by James Millikin, a young livestock and land dealer from Pennsylvania. Millikin had amassed a fortune of $75,000 by the age of 29. Recognizing his business acumen Decatur businessmen asked the young entrepreneur to organize a bank. Over the years the bank had prospered by providing loans to a city with a growing economy. Millikin Bank was recognized in the early 1900s as one of the strongest banking institutions in the state outside of Chicago.

Millikin's profits also enabled him to found the university that bears his name. A philanthropist, he donated hundreds of thousands of dollars to various charities.

At his death in 1909 Millikin's will gave control of the bank to a charitable trust. That trust came to an end in 1984 when Magna Group Inc. of Belleville, Illinois, a bank holding company, purchased Millikin National. Having foresight, James Millikin had empowered the trustees of the bank to sell "any and all" of the shares "when in their best judgment such sale would be for the best interest of the estate entrusted to their keeping." The Millikin National Bank became Magna/Millikin National Bank of Decatur in 1987. Currently, the bank goes under the name of Magna Bank of Central Illinois. Officers listed in the 1994 city directory include: Corydon C. Nicholson, community president; Randall W. Richardson, senior vice president; Jim D. Miller, Larry D. Anderson, Brian K. Brace, Phillip R. Curr, and Wilbur R. Lancaster, vice-presidents.

James Millikin was of strict Scotch Presbyterian ancestry. Millikin's first trip to the Midwest was in 1849 when he and his father drove a flock of sheep to Indiana and sold them at a profit. The next year James returned with livestock to Danville, Illinois. He began to buy property in the area and continued to buy and sell livestock. In 1856 he made the move to Decatur and founded his bank in 1860.

Millikin National Bank's second home, from 1880-1894, was located at the corner of East Main and Water.

The main banking floor of the newly constructed Millikin National Bank in 1896.

Conducting bank business in the lobby of the new facility at 100-104 North Water Street in 1925.

The 1896 Millikin National Bank facility, distinguished by its terra cotta style, was referred to as the "most pretentious" office building in downstate Illinois.

First of America Bank

Citizens National Bank opened its door in 1883 as a private banking firm ran by J. R. Gorin, J. A. Dawson and L. B. Casner. This enterprise organized in a room in the central block, but business grew so rapidly that the cashier, J.A. Dawson, negotiated the purchase of a lot at the corner of East Prairie and Merchant where a handsome building was raised. In 1910 Citizens moved to its present quarters in the 200 block of North Water Street.

In 1891 with capital of $100,000 it was decided to incorporate as a national bank. By 1892 Citizens National capital had doubled.

Many "firsts" distinguished the banking house. In 1902 Citizens opened the first savings department in the city. Another first included the Christmas Savings Club started in 1913. William Barnes, Jr., organized the first farm service department in 1928 and in 1930 the bank began the process of photographing checks in order to have a permanent record. The bank had the first night depository to enable businessmen to drop off deposits before or after banking hours. Citizens was the first bank in Illinois to establish a payment loan department to make direct loans for cars, homes, personal loans, etc. in 1934. 1954 saw the first curb teller for auto banking built and in 1960 Citizens became the first downstate Illinois bank to establish a common trust fund.

Most of us are very familiar with ATM's (Automatic Teller Machines), and Citizens was the first bank in the United States to purchase one such machine in 1972.

Citizens, along with Springfield banks, established the "Easy Answer" automatic teller machines in 1982. The bank merged with the Midwest Financial Group, Inc. in 1983 and in 1989 Citizens National Bank became affiliated with First of America Bank of Kalamazoo, Michigan.

The bank celebrated its first one hundred years in 1991 with assets totaling $256,687,000 and capital of over $18,000,000. Eleven men have served in the capacity of president since its founding. They are Jerome R. Gorin, Lewis B. Casner, Milton Johnson, Henry Schlaudeman, Robert Hunt, J. A. Corbett, A. M. Kenney, William Barnes, Jr., J. H. Crocker, J. L. Hunter, William Barnes III and current president, Phillip C. Wise. First of America Bank remains committed to the Decatur area and the concept of community banking.

Original bank lobby 1909-1936. The building was expanded and completely renovated beginning in 1946.

The bank's bunting and outside decorations took first prize in the August 1912 homecoming (comparable with today's Decatur Celebration).
Platforms were erected for concerts, parades and horse races with a calendar of the day's events featured in the *Daily Review*.

Top left: The ladies' room in the earlier bank, 1909-1936. During that era it was common to provide women separate areas in common facilities like train depots and hotel parlors to afford them greater comfort and privacy.

Top right: All windows are busy including the loan payment line on Saturday morning May 29, 1948.

Citizens National Bank going up in 1910 at the corner of Water and North Park streets.

Citizens National Bank installed the weather tower on top of the building on August 1, 1971. The tower was remotely controlled by WSOY Radio around the clock with the tower lights indicating the weather forecast for the next 24-hour period. The "Big C" came down in early 1990.

Department Stores in Decatur

Decatur's first general store was started in 1833 by William Cantrell on the southwest corner of Lincoln Square. The city's first major department store, however, did not arrive on the scene until 1859–Morehouse and Wells on East Main Street. Linn & Scruggs, established in 1869, foiled its competition by succeeding for over a century.

Decatur has long been a furniture retailing center: Bachman Furniture in 1880, Scovill's in the 1890s, Quigle Furniture and Henry Bachrach's were other noted dealers. Dime stores and chain stores all made their mark in the early part of the 20th century.

Retail stores operating here in the 1900s included many national firms: Sears Roebuck and Company, Montgomery Ward and J.C. Penney. Sears after using smaller quarters for a period, moved in 1941 into a new building at North and Franklin streets. This became the public library when Sears in 1966 erected a larger building in the 200 block of North Franklin. In 1966 Montgomery Ward, once an 1870s Chicago-based mail order house, moved into "commodious" quarters at the foot of South Water Street. In 1948 J.C. Penney opened a store at North and Water streets; the firm is now at the Hickory Point Mall in Forsyth.

After operating as separate department stores for many years, the firms of William Gushard and H.S. Gebhart merged in 1932. Block & Kuhl, which had come to Decatur in the mid-1920s, bought the building in 1950. In 1965 the Block & Kuhl corporation merged with the Chicago-based Carson Pirie Scott which used this location until 1979 when it also moved to Hickory Point Mall.

Decatur, like many other cities, finds its downtown district hard hit by shopping centers.

First of these centers was Colonial Mall, developed in 1948 at Grand Avenue and Route 48. This was followed in 1956 by The Pines at William and 22nd streets; Fairview Plaza at Fairview Avenue and King Street in 1958; South Shores in 1961, south of the Franklin Street bridge; Northgate Mall, between North Water Street and Broadway near Pershing Road in 1970 and the Mt. Zion shopping center on Route 121 near Route 36 in 1975. Hickory Point Mall is by far the largest, and the others almost help the downtown stores compete with it.

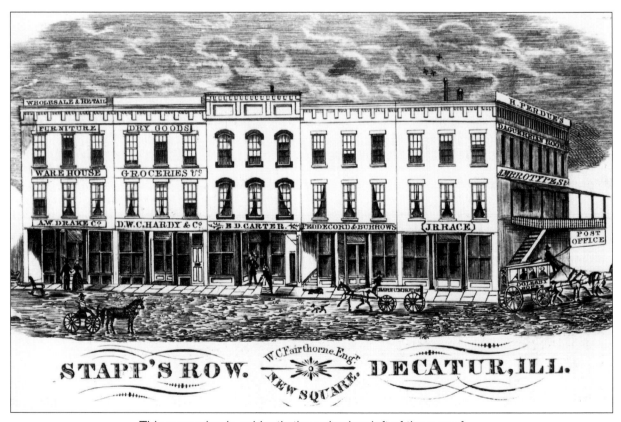

This engraving is evidently the only view left of the row of five store buildings built by Dr. James Stapp and E.O. Smith in the early 1860s on what is now South Park Street. The block was three stories high and was recognized as the exclusive place to shop during and after the Civil War era.

Turn-of-the-century
Morehouse and Wells Store
at 134 East Main Street.

113

Morehouse and Wells

W. T. Wells and S. P. Morehouse founded the retail business of Morehouse and Wells in 1859. They were dealers in hardware, stoves, furnaces, mantels, guns, and sporting goods. The first company store was at 7 East Main Street but moved to 134 East Main Street in 1884. When the block burned to the ground in 1909 a similar structure was erected on the same site and business resumed in 1912. In 1931, Morehouse and Wells became the first ground floor tenant in the new Citizens office building at Water and William streets, but in 1937 moved to the Standard Building at West Main and Water streets where it stayed until 1948. In 1948, the store was moved again to the northwest corner of Franklin and William streets where a fire on New Years Day of 1958 ended the company's retail reign just short of the hundred-year mark. The wholesale business, however, continued until 1975 in the 800 block of North Morgan Street.

View of the interior of the enlarged Morehouse and Wells at 134 East Main Street.

Morehouse & Wells was, in fact, the second oldest, continuously operated business house in town and is antedated only by the Michl Tobacco Company which was founded one year earlier in 1858. Partners and presidents through their 99-year history included C.M. Hurst, H.H. Bishop and Bob and Wilbur Humphrey.

Photo at right displays some of the hardware for which Morehouse and Wells was famous. In later years they added a line of home appliances.

Old-timers will remember when the store's local hauling was done in shiny wagons pulled by a handsome pair of draft horses. In 1884 the retailer had moved from a small storefront to "commodious" quarters in a new six-story edifice (photo right).

Linn & Scruggs

Linn & Scruggs was a major Decatur department store for over a century. It was established as a dry goods store in 1869 on Merchant Street on the square. About ten years later it moved to the southeast corner of West Main and Water streets where it survived two fires. The retailer moved into the Bachman Building at Main and Prairie in 1924 where it stayed until acquired by Myers Brothers in 1970. Linn & Scruggs finished its career in the former Montgomery Ward space in the 300 block of North Water Street.

Pictured is Linn & Scruggs' second emporium raised on the southeast corner of Main and Water. Linn & Scruggs vacated the structure to Henry Bachrach's discount store, Cheap Charley's. The store was rebuilt after a 1909 fire. Scovill Furniture, founded by Guy N. Scovill, was established in the late 1880s on the same site.

William R. Scruggs, who, along with W.H. Linn, established the Linn & Scruggs dry goods firm on Merchant Street in 1869. When the company opened a one-room location and began to undersell the competition, they were labeled a "fly-by-night" store that would not last the year.

Linn & Scruggs in October 1969, at Main and Prairie streets. The firm also opened a satellite store at South Shores Shopping Center in 1962.

The decision to move to Main and Prairie was made by J.R. Holt, a great-nephew of W.R. Scruggs and T.J. Prentice who had bought the store from the W.H. Linn heirs and from Scruggs in 1907. Holt retired as president of the company after holding that position for 30 years in 1965.

115

Neustadt's, a retail store, located in downtown Decatur for many years, was a clothing store that operated on the northwest corner of North Water and Prairie streets. It closed circa 1943.

Above: The Gebhart and Sessel's stores at Water and William streets in downtown Decatur on February 2, 1934.

Below: The H.S. Gebhart Company store before its merger with Gushard's. Judging by the crowds in many photos, the retail trade was one of the major draws to downtown Decatur throughout the first half of the 20th century.

The William Gushard and H. S. Gebhart stores had operated on opposite corners of Water and William streets for 25 years when they merged in 1932. The Gebhart store moved in with the Gushard store at that time and it became Gebhart-Gushard. In the mid-1940s the store was acquired by Aldens, but there was no name change until Block & Kuhl bought the business from Aldens in 1949. Block & Kuhl was located in the Standard Building at West Main and Water streets when it first came to Decatur in the mid-1920s. It then took over the vacated Gebhart building at Water and William streets in 1932. After Block & Kuhl acquired the seven-story Gebhart-Gushard building across the street, Neumans apparel store moved into the vacated Block & Kuhl building (previously the Gebhart store). Circa 1965, Block & Kuhl merged with Chicago-based Carson Pirie Scott and operated under that name.

Neuman's, a women's clothing store located on the southwest corner of North Water and William streets in August 1950. Ready-made women's wear had become big business since the 1920s. Once the "modern" woman was free from making all the family's wardrobe she never looked back.

The closing of Stauber's Department Store. It was established by a group of buyers and department heads who left Gebhart-Gushard's after it was acquired by Alden's in 1945. Under the leadership of Robert Stauber, it occupied space in the Standard Building where it continued in business until its demise in September 1968. Stauber's was the last locally owned department store in Decatur.

The card section of Haines and Essick on May 21, 1962. Harry Haines was a co-founder of the business in 1902. Haines and the late W. R. Essick established the firm as a book store in the 100 block of East Prairie Avenue. W.M. Weck assumed ownership and the position of general manager in 1936. In 1948 Richard K. Corlett merged with Haines & Essick, Inc. In December 1955, a group of investors, headed by Richard K. Corlett bought controlling interest in Haines & Essick, Inc., from W. Meredith Weck.

J. C. Penney's

The exterior of the "brand new, coming soon" (see notices in windows) J.C. Penney store at 310 North Water Street on April 24, 1926. In response to the chain store movement, James Cash Penney opened his first store in Kemmerer, Wyoming in 1902 and kept building.

The new downtown Penney's building at 410 North Water Street on November 15, 1948 shortly after construction. The site was once home to the J.R. Race mansion erected in 1870-71. The plot of ground it stood on was cut up into 11 lots. Guy Scovill and H. Warnecke bought the property in 1915 and built the one-story businesses which were razed to make way for Penneys.

Men employees of the J.C. Penney Company were wearing bright blazer smocks in this photograph on February 29, 1952, when women employees ran the store for two days. The two female managers on this leap-year day were Dorothy Miller and Cecile Snyder.

This 1968 photo shows Sears & Roebuck erected at North and Franklin streets just before World War II. The Decatur Public Library currently has its home in this facility and the Sears store moved to larger quarters at 130 North Franklin Street. Sears currently remains downtown. Relocation of the Sears store in the area between Franklin Street and Broadway and Prairie Avenue and East Main Street brought back a touch of the glory days when the Revere Hotel on that site enjoyed business prominence 100 years earlier. When the Revere House stood at the corner of Franklin Street and Prairie Avenue, the northwest corner of the new Sears site, the area bustled with business activity and notables. Abraham Lincoln, Stephen A. Douglas and others would stop at the Revere House during the circuit-riding court days.

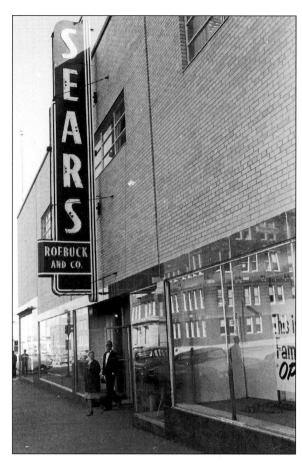

Part of the opening day crowd of 10,000 customers is shown beyond the check out counters in the new Kresge store at 337-355 North Water Street. The new store opened on March 15, 1959 with ribbon-cutting ceremonies attended by Mayor Clarence A. Sablotny. In the right foreground, H. L. Annesly, store manager, checks some records with Mrs. Edgar Liesman, a cashier. Kresge's first Decatur listing was at 315-317 North Water Street with J. L. Pickering serving as manager. In 1977 the firm closed at 343 North Water Street.

The smart new 56-stool lunch counter in the newly opened Kresge store in March of 1959. The modern stainless steel kitchen which served the lunch counter was on the floor above it. However, the lunch counter did not replace the snack bar which was such a popular feature in the old Kresge store. A brand new snack bar was on the opposite side of the building.

This photo is believed to be of the Ullrich Brothers market at 144 East Main in 1884. Peter Ullrich ran the brothers' retail operation at this address while brother, John, was in charge of the wholesale trade at 248 East Main.

Grocery Stores

In early Decatur a cow pastured at the edge of town was a common way for families to supplement grocery needs. Fresh foods were available at a grocer's downtown, with items taken in trade i.e. deer meat or fur pelts in exchange for eggs and butter. For over a hundred years the Decatur grocer knew his customers by name and whether he should extend credit to them or not. By the Civil War canned goods had appeared. By the late 1800s introduction of gas and electric coolers allowed grocers and meat markets to provide more variety. Only after World War II was there the most dramatic change: with metals available the food industry boomed with canned goods, not to mention pre-packaged foods. Refrigerators with freezers were found in most homes removing the daily shopping jaunt. Chain stores and self-service were the next order of the day. Gone was the day when the grocer home delivered your order or measured out the exact number of Hydrox cookies for your family's dinner table.

An 1896 photograph of the Temple Block with a horse-drawn Family Grocery wagon parked out front of the store. The advertising sign on the wagon says the store was at 337 North Water Street and it sold both foreign and domestic fruits and vegetables. The store also wanted its customers to know that it had recently acquired a new telephone number.

The C.F. Sterr building at 535-537 North Morgan Street which housed the R.H. Edwards Meat Market.

Early Stores in Decatur

It is impossible to note in consecutive order the establishment of stores in Decatur or even to name all of the stores of the log cabin period. If we are to credit the Abe Lincoln "Navigation of the Sangamon" speech, I.C. Pugh had a store on West Main street in 1830. It would appear from the context to have been in the 200 or 300 block. It was in front of this store that General Whitesides and Abraham Lincoln made their speeches, therefore there had to be such a store. [E.T. Coleman]

Lloyd W. Snerly Select Groceries at North Main and William streets. This building was occupied later by Greider's Cafeteria, a popular Decatur restaurant.

The interior of a typical corner grocery store before the advent of the supermarket. The homey atmosphere and the pyramid can displays are seldom found in today's self-service world. Ways of doing business were different from 1900 to circa 1930. The customer handed the grocer her list and he filled each item from behind the counter. Often he needed no list but had the customer's needs well remembered.

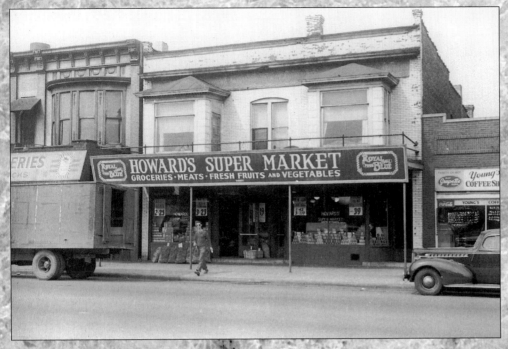

Howard's Super Market on March 15, 1948, located at 1136 East Eldorado Street was called a super market in name only. However, in many stores self-service was on the rise.

Old-timers may remember one of the region's first semi-trucks in the post-Depression era delivering groceries to Piggly Wiggly at Cantrell and Jasper. This picture is dated November 21, 1942. Albert Eisner had opened his chain of grocery stores at the turn of the century and adopted the name Piggly Wiggly. His 1920s slogan was "We help those who help themselves." The Piggly Wiggly chain got its start in Champaign, Illinois.

Pictured is the Eisner Grocery Store in September 1952. Even when the Piggly Wiggly name was changed to Eisner, many Decatur residents preferred the more colorful moniker.

The Parlor Market downtown in post-war Decatur on April 5, 1947. Located on the corner of North Main and West Main, it had the distinction of advertising at two addresses—at 103 North Main, where El Dora Fashions is now, and 130 West Main, which is currently vacant. The Parlor opened in 1899 as a meat market with proprietors A. E. Mott and Frank E. Goodman. This corner store closed in 1948 with John E. Keene listed as the last owner.

The National Food Store on Broadway (now Martin Luther King, Jr. Drive) later became the IGA. That building now houses the Knights of Columbus Hall. Local grocers succumbed to national chains circa 1910. Chains bought in bulk, offered lower prices, variety, wide aisles and eventually parking lots. Family-owned businesses retreated to cater to the smaller neighborhood market.

125

Beer - Beer - Beer

The last beer to be made in Decatur came out of the old brewery on the corner of Cantrell and Broadway (now Martin Luther King, Jr. Drive) in 1914. Started in 1856, the brewery was originally known as the Decatur Brewing Company, before becoming over the years Blue Ribbon Malt Extract, Premier Malt Products and finally the property of Premier-Pabst Corporation of Milwaukee, Wisconsin.

Lack of switching lines near the brewery led to the plant's demise. Company officials worked with the Illinois Central officials to try to get tracks to negotiate track access, however, the physical obstacles were insurmountable. The cost to bring raw materials to the brewery and to ship the finished product, thus, was prohibitive. Operations at the brewery were discontinued in 1930.

The Decatur Brewing Company in 1908, located at 646-611 East Cantrell Street, was organized by John Koehler and Adam Keck. At 15,000 barrels a year, the company boasted itself the city's largest.

By 1920 the Volstead Act had stopped the flow of beer and barrels. During Prohibition Premier Malt met the demand for products used in the making of home brew. Early brewers roll out the barrel in Decatur circa 1890 (photo right).

Plant number 1 of the Premier Malt Products Company. Frank and Harry Shlaudeman were the sons of Henry who had incorporated Decatur Brewery in 1888. The Shlaudeman family operated the firm through Prohibition. Shortly before the ratification of the 21st Amendment, the plant changed its name to Blue Ribbon Malt Extract and then was absorbed by Pabst in 1932.

Wet vs Drys

Cries of the "demon drink" by the Women's Christian Temperance Union and by families were heard across America at the turn of the century. In Decatur the slogan was "Girls are Worth More Than Saloons." The battle was on: The Wets vs the Drys.

In 1908, with 64 saloons in the city, the "wets" were slow to get worried when the "drys" took after them. The saloon-keepers even continued to laugh about the whole thing when Evangelist Billy Sunday came to town to join the fight. When he started lambasting booze and the men who sold and drank it gave the city a terrifying jolt.

The election came and the saloons were voted out by a plurality of 1,048 votes.

Shortly thereafter, a reporter for a Chicago newspaper, telling of his visit to Decatur, said he found more than 50 "blind pigs" selling drinks—that he could get a drink in Decatur as easily as in Chicago.

Perhaps some of the Billy Sunday converts were backsliders. Perhaps the "wets" put on a harder campaign. The "wets" won the next election by a margin of 531 votes.

But four years later the city went dry again by 1,762 votes and in 1916 voted dry again by 1,598 votes.

Then came Prohibition in 1920. [E.B. Hitchcock]

The Emerald Inn in 1934 sold burgers and beer (cost—five cents) and it was open all night. Located at 2703 North Water, the site is currently surrounded by Sherwin Williams and Seno Formal Wear. The Bridal Suite can also be found there at 2705 North Water.

The long-time popular Garfield Tap at 849 East Garfield in August 1951. The tavern was located next to the ICGRR tracks south of the Garfield Overpass. The current address is 1937 North Railroad Avenue. Garfield Tap was no longer in business by 1993 according to the City Directory.

Brought Whiskey

In 1858 Abraham Miller hauled a wagon load of goods from Springfield to Decatur for the Stamper & Condell store. "And I brought back a barrel of whisky for Berry Cassell," he added. "It was quite the common thing for well-to-do men to have a barrel in their cellar and nearly all stores kept a barrel of whisky on tap. That same year he recalled taking a two-bushel sack of corn to the little distillery at what was then called "Yaller Gall Spring," bringing back a gallon of whisky, which he had got for his corn. [E.T. Coleman]

Interior shot of men relaxing at the Pleasure Inn in February 1950. Located on the edge of town at 3701 East William, it was a night-club in the late 1940s that became a men's hangout in the 1950s. The current site is the approximate home of Creekmur Muffler and Brakes. The neighborhood was formerly known as "Junior Junction."

Bush's Tavern at 2775 East William. Reportedly, once a "bootleg" place where you could dine, dance and buy gas in September 1942. The William Street Reservoir and Fire Station Two now occupies the site.

The Transfer Tap in February 1951 at 118 North Merchant Street. The Tap was known to have "A dice game or two going upstairs." The building is now home to Robbie's Restaurant.

Esker's Tavern

The building that houses Esker's Tavern was originally built by Don Carter, and started life as Galka's Grocery. Otto "Cowboy" Star opened it as a bar, having received one of the first ten liquor licenses issued after Prohibition was repealed. He owned it until he went off to war and his wife Mabel "sold it out from under him" to Elmer Welch and Vic Esker circa 1941.

While the war was on, the new tenants moved the bar inside the building from the east to the west side of the room while the building was being jacked up and the basement dug. It was called Elmer's until 1949 when Welch sold out to Vic, who then took on his brother and former bartender, Arthur "Speed" Esker, as his partner. Vic sold his interest to Speed in the 1960s, and Speed ran the bar until selling to Pat Nolan in the mid-1970s.

Ensuing owners included, in the '70s, Angelo Drakos, Steve Grimm and Don Crissup. Joe and Lois Brandis took charge in the '80s until they sold it to Doug Burrows, the present owner, in 1991.

Esker's Tavern has been a landmark at 1703 East Clay for many years. In this picture, the bar was still on the east side of the building.

The bar was moved to the west side to accommodate access to the basement that was dug to provide storage. Beer kegs were then tapped in the basement rather than being stored behind the bar.

Esker's in its pre-basement era. It is a friendly neighborhood bar that has long been known for good food and a friendly atmosphere.

Hangouts

Many Decatur residents reminisce about the good times they had at after school hangouts or favorite night spots. Names like the Taco Box, the Shore and Perry's Drive-In evoke memories from the 1950s. In the '30s some may remember there was a "speakeasy" in the Prohibition era on the northeast corner of Route 36 and Country Club Road on the lake. Later the place became the Navy Club, owned by Commandant Harvey Warnick. The club sported tiki torches and was famous for dancing and big name bands.

The Pompon at 1098 West Wood, managed by William C. Newton, drew the high school crowd in the '40s and '50s. Don't forget the Wayside Inn across the street from the Stephen Decatur High School at the mid-century mark. The Millikin kids went to the Blue Mill with its big bar that featured names like the Ink Spots in the '40s and where a student taking a break could order a juicy hamburger, cole slaw with fries for $1.00 or all the shrimp you could eat for under a dollar. The Winery hasn't changed much. The great Winery burger is still attracting the Millikin crowd. In the '40s and '50s the jukebox and pool room as well as the Polish sausage were also popular. Some remember Payne's Supper Night Club from the '40s through the '60s at 233 North Main where Gene Bell played the piano and organ. And the list goes on.

Hue (Samuel Houston) Singleton, the first African-American restaurant owner in Decatur, came to town when E.G. Egbert bought the Revere House. Egbert brought Singleton with him from Iowa to work as a bellhop and waiter at the Revere. In 1884, a proprietor who had been operating a poorly patronized restaurant on the northwest corner of Lincoln Square disappeared. Singleton bought the building, cleaned out the cockroaches, hired one of the best cooks in the city and his clientele grew as the word spread about the good food. He operated his restaurant for 37 years, selling in 1921. Upon retirement he lived in a handsome home on West McKinley Avenue until his death in March 1926 at the age of 77.

Inside Hue Singleton's restaurant on the northwest corner of Lincoln Square.

The Coffee Pot restaurant on Route 121 east of Lake Decatur in October 1929. This unusual structure is remembered by longtime Decatur residents. The identity of the couple in the photo is not known.

Great ice cream and good times were found at Goltermann's Ice Cream Garden; photo taken in August of 1947. Goltermann's, Inc. Ice Cream Manufacturers was at 1101 North Fairview Avenue. This address no longer exists, but as a point of reference, the address for MacArthur High School is 1155 North Fairview.

H. R. Greider makes change for a customer. Greider's Cafeteria was a good place to meet friends and in August of 1939 when this photo was shot it was a great place to lunch and catch up on war news in Europe.

An exterior shot of Greider's in 1960, the year it closed. Dominating the corner at 259 North Main Street, this restaurant is still remembered by a host of Decatur natives. The downstairs offered a buffet but for special occasions one went upstairs to enjoy fancy salads, silver service and an enticing fountain with colored lights to enchant the children. Macon Music later set up shop in this corner location.

Do you remember Dewey's Dine-A-Mite Restaurant in August of 1954? It was at 865 East Wood, which is now the home of McNamara Floor Covering.

Elmer's Variety Store, at 638-640 East Eldorado Street from 1946-1962, also included a popular lunch counter. The variety store went out of business due to competition from the new outlying shopping centers, especially Shopper's World at Brettwood Village. Elmer's was owned by Elmer and Sophia Coventry.

The Blue Mill name was a tribute to the Big Blue Millikin Sports team. The roots of the restaurant were planted in 1915 at 129 South Oakland by George Zeller who relocated in the '20s to the present site at Wood and Oakland. From 1926 until postwar the confectionery was known as the Blue Mill Tea Room. In the "Roaring Twenties," hamburgers cost 10 cents and drinks a nickel. It became the chief hangout for Millikin students. And for everyone when in 1934 air conditioning was installed—the only such building south of Kankakee with the exception of the theaters. A dance floor was added, pinball machines and WSOY broadcasted Dinner at the Mill in the '40s with Downey Hughey. After a fire destroyed the restaurant in April 1956, it reopened with a new Carousel Room by August. The Gold Room was added in 1962. H. J. McNamee of the "Brock (M. Braucher) and Mac" team sold his interest in 1967 after a 40-year reign. Don E. McKinney handed over the reins to Jim and Colleen Keyes in May of 1989.

The Shore Restaurant and Drive-in was an appealing Decatur eatery. This photo is from September of 1962. There is now a bait and tackle shop at this site which is located across from the entrance to Nelson Park at Cantrell and Lake Shore Drive.

Read's Cafe in April 1947 was located at 240 North Park building. This corner restaurant and gathering place was first home to the Manhattan Cafe in 1929 and was run by C. T. Pearson during the Depression and by Mrs. Shirley Whitney and Cleta Andrews afterwards.

The Spanish Inn on August 27, 1942 served customers at 732 South Jasper. This location became the Piggly Wiggly store by the end of 1943, and the address is now on Cantrell Street The building, though changed through renovations, remains standing.

Known as the Tick-Tock Drive Inn or Sandwich Shop or just plain Tick-Tock, it was located next to the Garment Workers building at 540 North Main. The site is the current home to a First of America Bank branch. Owners and managers from the post-Depression '30s through the mid '50s have included Joseph Keller, Fred and Emmy Burchard, Theo Burt, Harry and Mrs Iva Upton and Daniel Caulkins III. Renamed the Hi-Hat, the grill took on a new owner, Paul Mitchell, in 1958.

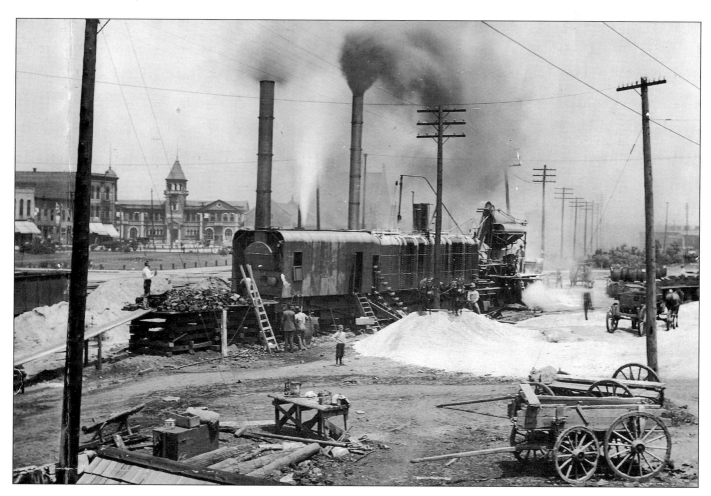

Streicher's Asphalt plant in 1912 set up north of Eldorado and east of the Illinois Central. All of the machinery pictured moved from city to city by rail originating out of Lima, Ohio. The smokestacks rested on hinges run out by conveyors and connected to the boilers. This portable plant produced road making material—2,000 square yards of asphalt two-inches thick every ten hours. The asphalt came from Bakersfield, California and was mixed with limestone dust added to four daily carloads of sand. To operate the plant required 150 tons of coal per week. The finished product came out from the boiler then was conveyed by pipes to, in this case, Eldorado Street. A wagon load of product was turned out every ten minutes. Streicher also was contracted to lay down asphalt on East Cerro Gordo.

E-Z Opener Bag factory moved to Decatur from Taylorville, Illinois in 1911. Makers of the "Oak" Brand of paper bags, the company distributed various sizes nationally, employing 150 workers with an annual payroll of $75,000. The site was at East William and North Broadway (now Martin Luther King, Jr. Drive). In 1916, the company moved to a new factory at 705 North Pine Street. The building was then taken over by the Hamman Brothers Moving and Storage Company, and E-Z Opener was closed in 1928.

Workers take a break for the photographer while loading the finished product from the company's freight dock at the East William Street location in 1911.

Still in existence today are the Illinois Power yard (bottom left), First of America Bank (the two dominant structures at top right of the photo) and St. James School, south of the bank. The photo was taken, it appears, from a hillside tower which no longer exists.

C.A. HUPP TOBACCO CO.

Bachman Furniture was established in 1880 by Charles Bachman. It became Bachman Brothers when Charles took his brother, William G., into the business. Their first big store was at North Main and Prairie streets. That building was later used by Linn & Scruggs and Quigle

Furniture. The Bachmans erected this retail house circa 1886 (photo) after the Temperance Tabernacle on that site was torn down. Bachman's sold furniture and stoves. In 1955 furniture was still sold from this site at 240 East Main by People's Furniture. A parking lot graces the location today.

The C. E. Ward Company, wholesale and commission, at 700 East Cerro Gordo in 1913. The wholesaler was first listed in the 1903 City Directory at 730-736 East Cerro Gordo with Charles E. Ward as designated owner. A wholesale fruit company it remained in business until 1956.

Schaffer & Gluck (originally Schaffer and Ringler) Furrier at 253 North Main was remodeled at a cost of $7,500 in 1937 (photo) to accommodate cold air storage with a capacity of near 2,000 coats. Furnishings for the remodeled store were provided by Bachman Company, and Lyon Lumber designed the front. Charles Schaffer and Herman Ringler opened the fur store in Decatur in 1925 in second floor quarters at 152 East Main Street. Manuel Gluck, an immigrant from Poland, attended Decatur High School by day, and worked for his brother-in-law, Charles Schaffer by night. Gluck eventually taught the fur trade to his son, Henry. Joan Gluck Young, third generation, succeeds her father, Henry, in carrying on the family-owned and operated business.

Pictured is Manuel Gluck and Earl Lucas working on a fur machine in the 1940s.

Below: The grand opening of Schiff's Shoe Store became a reality on February 2, 1949 at 322 North Water Street. A temporary staff of 50 were on hand as well as William Schiff, of the Shoe Corp. of America. The shoe store carried 50,000 pairs of shoes, offered 90 chairs for adults and 12 for children. Two air conditioning units had been installed at each end of the store "for the comfort of shoppers."

Brick Industry

Brick manufacturing began in 1852 when William Martin set up a plant near Broadway and Decatur. Eventually 3,000 bricks were turned out daily. The Decatur Tile Company, managed by John G. Shea, supplied five million bricks to a Detroit paving firm in 1887 after a team of engineers and officials inspected Decatur streets and were impressed with the quality of the materials. Prominent in Decatur brick business were Conrad Ammann, and three Mattes brothers, Frederick, John and Edward.

Martin, Decatur's pioneer brick manufacturer, sold out to Ben Metz. When the clay beds wore out, the brick makers moved on to other sites or left the city. Clay beds were located in what is now Fairlawn Cemetery, Nelson Park and Lincoln Park.

This home of artistic design, brick veneer with Royal Rug brick work, and cement porch and steps is located on Park Drive.

This hollow tile home with Royal Rug brick work, cement porch and brick steps is on Lincoln Place. Average cost for this type of house was $3,000 in 1916.

An early photo of the Decatur Brick Manufacturing Company.

This substantial and attractive home, brick veneered with Royal Rug brick work, is located on South Edward Street.

Making Brick in Early Decatur

It was not many years till it was discovered that Illinois mud would make excellent brick and then houses with brick foundations and some with outer walls of brick began to appear. These early brick were not made of shale, which could be found almost anywhere in the timber.

Perhaps most important of all from city improvement standpoint was the paving program. While Decatur did not lead in paving with brick, it was one of the first cities. In 1886 Lincoln Square was paved with two courses of brick on a sand cushion. It was the wonder of all the neighboring cities.

That paving inaugurated a program that included all the business section with Decatur vitrified brick. Residential streets were fast being covered and in 1890 the paving program alone had cost $300,000, an unusual amount for cities in that day. [E.T. Coleman]

Hi Flier

Harvey Sellers, Sr. launched his Hi Flier business in the basement of his home in 1921. Sellers designed and built or modified existing equipment to meet his needs for the manufacturing process as well as inventing the "stick lock" to hold the kite sticks together. Each kite manufactured by the company carried the warning: "Do not fly with wire or metallic wrapped string" recognizing that kites were good conductors of electricity. During peak season, Hi Flier employed nearly 200 people. The Decatur plant was closed on April 24, 1981 and operations were moved to Penrose, Colorado. Many longtime Decatur residents grew up flying Hi Flier kites.

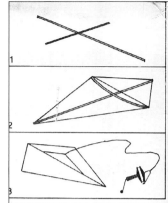

ISTRUCTIONS FOR TWO STICK KITE

1. Position Kite Sticks—Turn short cross stick at right angle to long upright stick. Slide cross stick and wire lock on upright stick until positioned properly to form kite. Insert string into notches at ends of cross sticks.

2. Attach Bow String—(backside of kite)—Tie a string taut between ends of the cross stick so that it bows about 6 inches.

3. Attach Bridle String—Tie a 24" string through holes in plastic to upright stick. Attach flying string to bridle string about 1/3 of the way down from the top.

How To Fly your Hi-Flier Kite—Hold flying string and run into the wind. Let out enough string until kite reaches desired height. No tail is needed in moderate wind. For best results, use Hi-Flier Kite Reel and Megalon kite cord.

CAUTION—DO NOT FLY KITES WITH WIRE OR METALLIC WRAPPED STRING

a Hi-Flier **EXCLUSIVE!**
Perfect for all kites

kite reel
(SPINWINDER™)

Action and control in launching and flying. Holds up to 1000 feet of cord. Protects hands from string burns.

The label from a Star Trek kite made by the Decatur Hi-flier kite company.

Worker sitting in the midst of a display of Hi-Flier kites.

Woman sands and finishes kite sticks at Hi-Flier.

"On sand lots in the cities, and in country pastures, they are sending them up, trying to keep them from doing tail spins and running 'messages to the clouds.' As the balmy winds of spring begin blowing the thoughts of the average small boy turns to kites."

From the day they opened in the early '20s Decatur-made kites reached the four corners of the USA *from five and dime stores in the country to department stores in the cities.*

The YMCA in Newark, New Jersey with 230 entrants reported that a Hi-Flyer kite rose high above them all in the national contest.

In 1926 five years after H. A Sellers organized Hi-Flier the company produced two million kites.

The company manufactured from August when it put back on a full workforce and works everyone hard into early spring. In the early years 50 girls worked in the second floor plant at the corner of Water and Marietta.

One of the firm's most popular styles was a 42-inch tail-less. Hi-Flier was also the exclusive dealer of duo-color kites.

Sellers traveled the USA promoting his products especially in the south. The staff he left in charge included John Hahn, Earl Frazier, Nellie Blanchard, Bernice Custer and longtime worker, Edna Sehlem. Often employees laid off from the previous spring returned to appreciative managers as lithe quick fingers were hard to train. [Herald & Review]

Kites are attached to the finished sticks.

All photographs are dated March 1938.

Two workers assembling Hi-Flier kites. Most of these appear to be Clippers, with balsa wood glider boxes at front right of the picture.

142

2525 East William Street. Kelso Fortner was the owner. The name was changed to Kelly Food Products in 1944. By 1954 Kelly had moved to 510 East Prairie and was owned by Isidor and S. Walter Tick.

According to Don Irwin, who worked for Crane for 40 years, the potato chip gained in popularity through promotion by salesmen. Originally the chip was only a summertime picnic popularity item. Then Chesty Potato Chip out of Terre Haute, Indiana began advertising at University of Illinois basketball games, increasing the demand. In order to get their chips into stores and restaurants, the salesmen had to carry and make available a host of other essential items on their trucks like canned pet food, chili, condiments and pretzels. Crane was the first to sell Wyler Lemonade on their trucks. The salesmen, along with selling other food items, pitched the potato chip as the perfect accompaniment to television snacking and viewing.

And the rest is history.

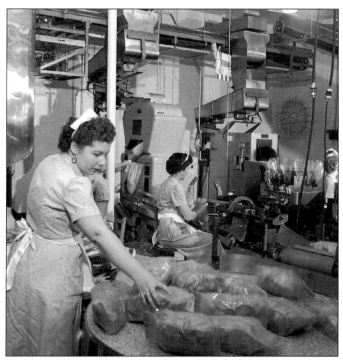

Bagging the finished product at the Perfect Potato Chip Company in March 1955.

The Perfect Potato Chip Company in March of 1955. Unloading potatoes in a hopper on their way to becoming a "perfect" chip.

Trucks lined up, loaded, and ready to deliver Crane potato chips in the late 1920s. Remember the baseball buttons inside the packages of Crane potato chips?

Sunshine Dairy

Lester P. Harder and C. A. Taylor opened the Taylor-Harder Dairy Company at 1020 North Summit Avenue in 1929. The firm was incorporated in April of 1946. In October of that year, Taylor and Harder purchased the interest of William S. Ridgly in the Ridglydale Dairy at 141 North Church Street. In 1948 Sunshine Dairy was formed by incorporating Taylor-Harder and Ridglydale, with Lester P. Harder as president. The latter celebrated a 42nd anniversary at its new plant at 725 East Prairie in 1971. At that time, it was the oldest dairy in Decatur. Sunshine got the "milk processed quicker and on to your favorite store or door." The dairy joined Prairie Farms in January 1987.

When Larry Taylor had decided to sell Sunshine Dairy to Prairie Farms in January of 1987, he completed 58 years of ownership by the Taylor family.

Delivery from Sunshine Dairy right to your door in the 1950s.

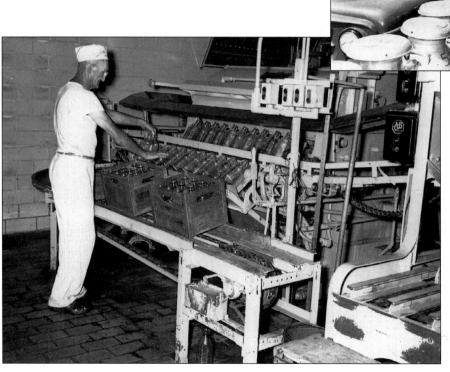

After pickup from farmers the raw product was unloaded at Sunshine Dairy. Milk used to be picked up from farmers twice a day, because they had no way to keep it cool. Notice the sign on the truck telling customers to "drink milk...it's good for you!"

Inside the Sunshine Dairy in the 1950s a dairy employee loads clean milk bottles into crates to reuse.

The Music Box sold musical instruments at 140 North Main. Mrs Marial Alltop and Glen E. Henson were the proprietors in 1955 (photo). By 1957 the firm had moved to 812 South 16th. A Music Box Cafe was added and run by Robert C. Workman. In 1960 only the cafe was still listed with Edna Atkins in charge. The location is now home to Pete Kate's Income Tax Service.

The Popular Fiddler
The only kind of musical instrument in the pioneer settlement was the fiddle. Our old time fiddler knew no notes but played by ear and much time was spent in learning the different popular tunes of the day. It goes without saying that the fiddler was always quite a social success in his home locality as he was always sure of an invitation to all of the parties that were held. If he were obliging he could usually furnish quite a bit of gossip gathered in his travels and acted as a kind of news gatherer for the different parts of the country. [E. T. Coleman]

Decatur Music Center was opened in 1945 by Mrs. Mabel Schultz joined by Louis and Ruth Beynon and Earl Huff, Jr. at 115 1/2 South Main (photo). In 1954 the center moved to 227 North Main. In 1958 Macon Music, Inc. (established in 1954) took over Decatur Music and the company prospered through changes of ownership, a move to Fairview Plaza, and its eventual demise in the mid-1980s. Macon Music, Inc. was THE place to go for sheet music, music instruments and lessons. Many remember giving recitals there, saving allowances to visit on Saturday mornings to pick from the vast array of sheet music available.

147

Daut's Greenhouses in July of 1951 were located off North Monroe Street and on Edword Street in the Monroe Park area. Jacob and Henry Daut, florists and gardeners, established a combination business and residence at the northwest corner of College and Harrison. The Park District purchased the land from F.J. and P.J Daut in 1948. The residence was moved by horse and wagon to 2081 North College Street. A member of the Daut family still resides there.

Pictured is the interior of Daut's greenhouse in early February 1937 in preparation for the busy and profitable Valentine's Day market. The neighborhood children were always made welcome, and often came away with "reject" plants in small clay pots. Daut's also grew plants to supply their own flower shop. Elizabeth Daut Dunn later owned and operated Betty & Bob's Florist.

Hinman Knitting Factory at 601 North Church in 1908. First listed in the 1901 City Directory at 133-137 North Main, the business was also located at 151 and 207 North Water. All locations produced dry goods, millinery, carpets, cloaks, suits, furs and hosiery. All the Hinman business ventures were headed up by Rolla P. Hinman. The Fixture Town currently occupies the site.

For many years Decatur has been the center of a varied pharmaceutical industry, employing highly skilled technicians. These firms have included Irwin-Neisler, Mallinckrodt Chemical Co., Taylor Pharmacal, Flint-Eaton and Lincoln Laboratories. Taylor Pharmacal Company is a Decatur manufacturer of pharmaceutical drugs for human and animal use. Taylor was founded in 1948 at 620 East Eldorado Street by the late Guy C. Taylor and his sons, Stanley and Ted. The company moved to a new building at 1222 West Grand Avenue in 1953. A new headquarters was erected at 150 South Wyckles Road in 1978. In 1989 the firm undertook a $750,000 remodeling project at the plant to further reduce chances that aseptically produced drugs could become contaminated. Pictured is an employee at Taylor Pharmacal Company in March 1958.

Bell's Drug at the corner of Main and North Streets in 1954. The structure was built in 1894 by the Loeb firm, which also supervised Millikin University's original construction. A distinctive architectural feature of the Bell building included the three turrets. Bell Drug was founded as a corporation on March 10, 1895 by the late H.W. "Doc" Bell. In 1935 Bell installed a 12-foot soda fountain. Numerous business owners, including Starbase 4 family amusement center and Franklin Fastprint, have occupied the 100-year-old site. Currently it belongs to A-1 Diamond and Gold Exchange.

Sol Tick and Company Scrap Iron. The firm has been in business in Decatur for over 50 years and is located at 1180 North 22nd Street. Sol Tick came to Decatur in 1937 as a young German immigrant. He engaged extensively in the junk business with his largest shipping yard doing business at the North 22nd Street site and one just east of the railroad tracks on East Eldorado. He was the downtown's premier landlord, owning considerable property for many years.

Founded by William G. Traver and G. M. Parish in 1926, the first plant at 1902 North Water was supposedly the first central mix concrete plant in central Illinois. That site became a block producing and materials plant and in 1954 the ready mix moved to 800 McKinley. In 1988 a new plant was raised at the latter address, and in 1994 the block manufacturing facility also moved to 800 McKinley. The plant has been sold several times over the years, although it has maintained the same name through the transitions. The enterprise is currently managed by Richard Goken, a previous owner, for Lone Star Industries of Stanford, Connecticut, which bought Traver circa 1990.

Traver Ready Mixed Concrete in August 1954. Gravel was sent on conveyor belts to a crusher as part of the concrete making process.

Adding the water and giving the end product a final stir before delivery.

In 1868 William Young and Fred Norman established the first steam laundry in the city and possibly in the state. In 1871 Young and Norman barbered at Six North Water Street. The laundry business had opened to accommodate the barber business as the washer people could not keep up with the volume. In 1910 Fred Norman, having bought out Young, operated a combination laundry barber shop with bath services and cigars sold at a 234 North Main location. In 1947 Norman Laundry & Dry Cleaning also offered cleaning, dyeing, hat blocking, rug shampooing and lace curtain work. Lorell and Nellie Sober served as officers of the firm just before the start of World War I and Glen and James Sober are current owners of Norman's Cleaners and Launderers at 145 East Decatur Street.

This was the first coin-operated dry cleaners in Decatur, according to Jim Sober, current owner of Norman's Dry Cleaners. It was identified as Brettwood Laundry and Dry Cleaning Village which opened in 1962 with John Kilborn as president. Home and coin-operated dry cleaning machines were not successful because of the regulations enforced against home and public use of the highly flammable solvents.

Decatur's Walgreen store in June of 1930 shortly after opening with C.W. Aldrich serving as manager at the 217 North Water location. The store closed in 1976.

Early Medicine

Taken over by E. A. West when he purchased the [Roberts Drug Store on Lincoln Square in the 1860s] thirty years ago, there were found in the basement odds and ends of old drug stock. These consisted mainly of jars of dried herbs that must have dated to the very beginning of things in Decatur. They were of no use to Mr. West except to clutter up space and were doubtless destroyed. But there is carefully preserved in this store a prescription book, the prescriptions written by the early doctors of the town, and they afford an interesting and valuable index [of early medicine]. [E.T. Coleman]

152

Downtown Decatur in 1957.

Decatur Bottling Works opened in 1929 at 604 East Cantrell and was owned by J. M. Scherer and C. P. Housum. In 1958 the business moved to 2090 East Olive with Merle R. Carroll taking over as president. The Bottling Works relocated in 1976 to 2112 North Brush College Road and is still in business. Pictured is the plant in July of 1953 at the corner of Cantrell and Broadway (now Martin Luther King, Jr. Drive).

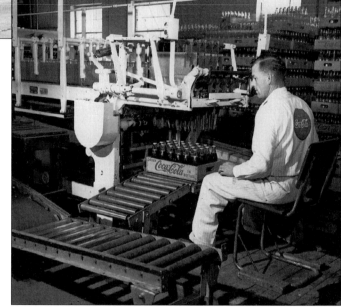

Early Road Maps

Road maps were published in those days and they were not greatly disimilar from the automobile trail maps published a few years ago. There was an 1851 little book known as "Colton's Western Tourist and Emigrant's Guide." This book was got out for the information of eastern people who were going west either as settlers or tourists. In this book is a good map of the stage roads. They were then called "Great Routes of Travel." The map was printed on good paper and the press-work was excellent.

But the interesting thing about this map is the fact that the "Great Routes of Travel," the state routes, were laid out upon lines that were followed substantially by the railroad lines subsequently built. These highways were laid out by good highway engineers, whether Indians or buffalo. [E.T. Coleman]

The Coca Cola Bottling Company was founded in 1909 at 543 South Franklin. The above photo was taken at the East Wood site in 1957.

Outside Rand McNally at 2044 Walnut Grove in January of 1958. McKeever Communications occupies the building at this time. Photo left: Working inside Rand-McNally in June of 1954.

154

Hayes Hatchery was torn down in the mid-'50s. Its insulated walls were used by Rex Cochran to build his Sealtest dairy cooler on Railroad Avenue.

Making the Sale at Hayes Hatchery in February of 1943.

Brothers Orville J. and Merle C. opened Hayes Brothers Hatchery behind Orville's residence in 1924 at 2039 North Monroe. The business later moved to 405 South Water Street where they used two giant mechanical mothers which had a capacity of 50,000 eggs each; 15,000 to 20,000 eggs hatched each week (photo left).

The local plant's two-story brick building housed a sales room, office, incubator room, box set-up assembly and a brooder room. The hatchery specialized in the filling of orders for day-old chicks.

The company was one of the largest, if not the largest, in Illinois, and yearly shipped chicks to every state.

K's Merchandise as it appeared in 1962, located in the Columbia Building at 322 Main Street. The business was founded in 1957 by the Eldridge family, Ray Eldridge, Sr., Vernice Eldridge, David Kay Eldridge and Ray Eldridge, Jr. David Kay Eldridge is the first and current president. Ray Eldridge, Jr., is the executive vice president. The original store was located on Main Street until it was destroyed by fire in 1968. K's then moved to their current Water Street location. In 1985, K's took possession of the building that was previously Carson Pirie Scott to house their sporting goods and toy departments.

They Don't Do Things That Way Anymore

Excavating a basement for construction of a building, while once done with horses and wagons as in this photo, it is done these days with more sophisticated machinery.

James J. Moran, a funeral home still in business today, was once known as an undertaker. He made his own coffins and had his own horse-drawn ambulances like the one pictured at right.

Bill Dietz, who sold coal oil and axle grease from his horse-drawn wagon, would find it difficult to make a living that way today.

Workers pluck and clean chickens at the Tick Produce Company. Burlap bags were worn to keep the workers' clothes tidy.

Like the present-day service station, the old horse-shoer and livery stable were a necessity in Decatur's horse and buggy era. In this photo it appears that a father was apprenticing a son in his trade.

Acknowlegements

A project like this one is never completed without help. Ours came from a variety of sources and in a variety of forms. People helped us out with encouragement, advice, the sharing of stories, the loan of treasured photographs, proofing and accuracy-checking. A special thanks to John Moorman, Decatur City Librarian, and the staff of the Decatur Public Library for support during the difficult production stages. Without the resources of the Decatur Public Library this publication would not have been possible. Appreciation also goes to First of America Bank for their recognition of the benefits of recording and preserving Decatur history. Thanks to Noel Dicks for his work in reproducing photos for the book. We would especially like to thank Mary Talbott of the Macon County Historical Society for her contributions.

We also extend our gratitude to all those who helped us out in so many ways, including:

Decatur Herald & Review
First National Bank
  of Decatur
Wagner Castings-
  Don Lawson
ADM - Karla Miller
Caterpillar Inc.-
  Angela Meyers,
K's Merchandise Mart-
  Jan Baughman
Jo Gluck Young
Thomas Garren
Colleen Keyes
Joan Bauer

Dorothy Shaw
Juanita Landers
Betty and Frank Trebacz
Shirley Edwards
Beverly Freeman
Don and Mike Irwin
Doug Imboden
Jim Sober
Mr. and Mrs. David Coventry
Elizabeth Dunn
Carolyn Cochran
Doug Burrows
Elmer Coventry
Jerry Bafford

Bibliography

Aldrich, Jack. *Decatur's Growth As a Railroad Centre 1854-1954. Before & After.* Jack Aldrich, Decatur, Illinois, 1994.

"Antebellum Decatur and Macon County 1816-1860". Heritage Committee, Inc., Decatur, Illinois, 1968.

Banton, O. T. *Decatur, Illinois.* Macon County Historical Society, Decatur, Illinois, 1983.

Banton, O. T. *History of Macon County,* 1976. Macon County Historical Society, Decatur, Illinois, 1976.

Clarke, S. J. *Past and Present of the City of Decatur and Macon County Illinois.* S. J. Clarke Publishing Co., Chicago, Illinois, 1903.

Coleman, E. T. *History of Macon County.* Review Publishing, Co., Decatur, Illinois, 1929.

Decatur City Directory. R. L. Polk and Co., Taylor, Michigan. Numerous years were consulted in the writing of this book.

Decatur Herald & Review newspaper articles & *Decatur Tribune* newspaper articles. Decatur, Illinois.

80 Years of Banking 1860-1940. Edited by O. T. Banton. Millikin National Bank, Decatur, Illinois, 1940.

Forrestal, Dan. *Kernel and the Bean.* Simon and Schuster, New York, New York, 1982.

Heimburger, Dan. *Wabash.* Heimburger House Publishing, Co., River Forest, Illinois, 1984.

History of Macon County, Illinois. Brink, McDonough and Co., Philadelphia, Pennsylvania, 1880. A reproduction of the original done by Whipporwill Publications, Evansville, Indiana, 1985.

Hitchcock, E. B. *Story of Decatur. Decatur Daily Review,* Decatur, Illinois, 1923-1926. Series of articles written for the newspaper.

Kahn, E. J. Jr. *Supermarketer to the World.* Warner Books, New York, New York, 1984.

Manufacturing and Mercantile Resources of the City of Decatur 1887-88. E. N. Baker Publishing Co., Decatur, Illinois, 1887.

Nelson, Hon. William E. *City of Decatur and Macon County Illinois,* Volumes 1 and 2. Pioneer Publishing Company, Chicago, Illinois, 1910.

Portrait and Biographical Record of Macon County, Illinois. Lake City Publishing Co., Chicago, Illinois, 1893.

Richmond, Mabel E. *Centennial History of Decatur and Macon County.* Decatur Review, Decatur, Illinois, 1930.

Smith, John. *History of Macon County Illinois From Its Organization to 1876.* Rokker's Printing House, Springfield, Illinois 1876.

Staley Journal. A. E. Staley Manufacturing Company, Decatur, Illinois, various issues in the Decatur Public Library's local history files.

Stringham, Paul. *Illinois Terminal: The Electric Years.* Interurban Press, Glendale, California, 1989.

Tanner, Helen Hornbeck. *Atlas of the Great Lakes Indian History.* University of Oklahoma Press, Norman Oklahoma, 1987.

"Then and Now, 1857-1957." Mueller Company Advertising Department, Decatur, Illinois, 1957.

Windish, Leo G. *Soybean Pioneers.* Leo G. Windish, Galva, Illinois, 1981.

Index

First of America Bank wishes to dedicate this publication to the people of Decatur, past and present, whose faith, courage and determination have helped build a strong foundation for our city's progress and growth.

160

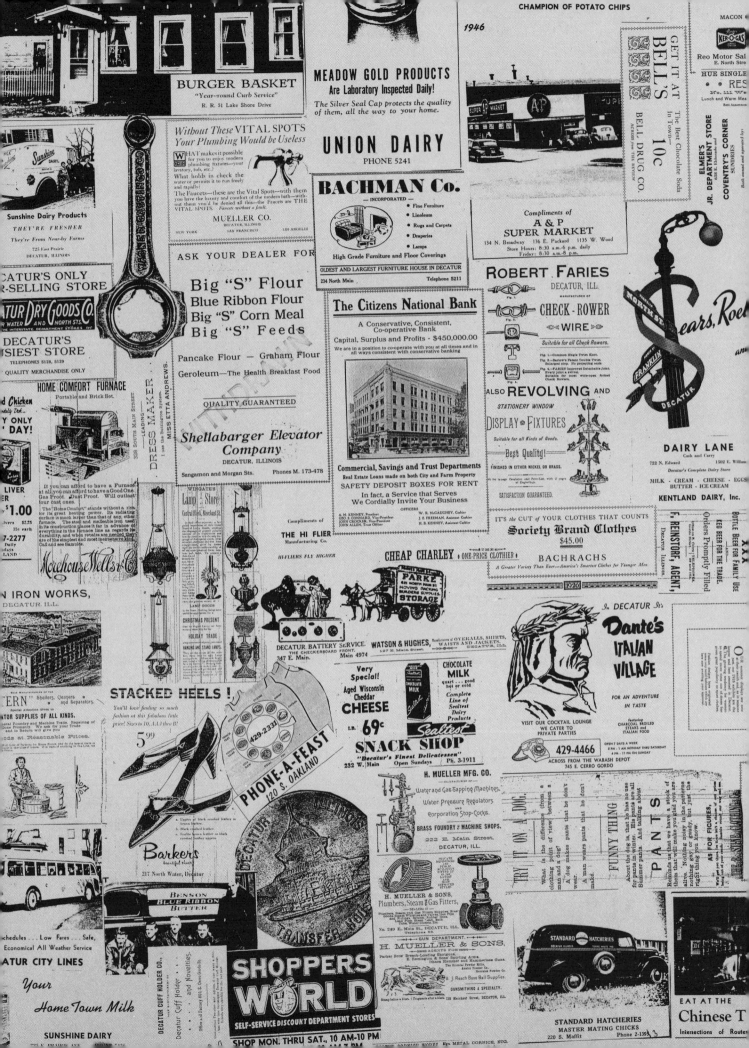